Acute Angles

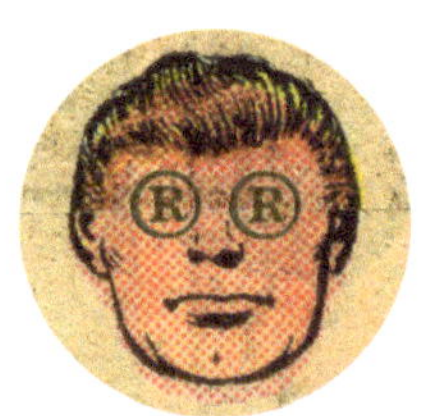

AUTHOR'S NOTE

I recently published a book entitled *We Said Hello and Shook Hands*, which featured more than 400 collages done in collaboration with other artists. In some cases they would give me collages they had started, and I would finish them. In other cases, I would create collages with the intention of handing them off to another artist to complete.

Fueled by my curiosity and excitement for the collage medium and the online community it supports, I quickly familiarized myself with many influential artists, styles and technique. I began using the start phase of the collaborative process for exploring new ways of working. Letting go of the responsibility for the finished outcome and focusing my attention solely on the starts, I started trying new things and finding out what I liked or disliked about the paper and the composition. I found myself paying more attention to details of materials, and exercising more restraint in terms of both the number and variety of elements in the collage.

When I first started collaborating, I had a hard time figuring out when to stop. I found it difficult to start an idea and stop halfway through, and often went too far. I began to see that putting too much into a starter collage narrows the options for the finisher. A starter collage that is free of detailed imagery and meaningful text gives the finisher more room to move: denuding the starter collage of all historical reminiscences opens up the possibilities for the finisher.

However, I found that this way of working opened up possibilities for me as well. I have come to enjoy the idea of visual purity or minimalism in my starter collages. Exploiting the formal and taking away the historicity results in work that, while more abstract and non-objective, is evocative and expressive in its own way. While these collages may have been created with the intention that they were not yet complete and would be added to and finished, it turned out that many of them can stand alone as resolved works of art.

That is the origin of *Acute Angles*, a collection of collages that, while originally intended to be taken over by someone else's voice, seemed to want to speak for themselves.

Zach Collins
March 2016

FOREWARD

I first ran across the collages in this collection on Zach's Tumblr site, where they were paired with other images as the "before" half of before-and-after collaborations between Zach and other artists. While I am all in favor of collaborative projects, I found that in almost every instance I actually preferred the freshness and openness of the "starter" collages to the more complex and often more literal imagery of the "finished" collaborations. I wrote to Zach to tell him so. We corresponded for a while, and eventually he invited me to help select and arrange the images which make up this book.

Collage is essentially the juxtaposition of elements. Putting two things next to one another creates a certain field of energy in the space between them. But the complexity of a collage grows exponentially as the number of elements increases. If there are two elements, they speak to one another: it's one conversation. If there are three elements, then there are three conversations. If four, then six. If five, then ten. And so on.

Artists throughout history have struggled with the question of how to know when a work is finished. (Leonardo da Vinci is supposed to have remarked that "A work of art is never finished, only abandoned.") For a collage artist, there's always a temptation to add just one more thing, but, as Zach has noted in his introduction, it can be dangerous to do so. Every artist has had the experience of going one or two steps too far and seeing a once-promising piece turn into a clotted mess. In painting, you can sometimes go back and paint over. But in collage, once something is glued down, the only way to get rid of it is to either rip it off or glue something else over it, either of which can make the problem even worse.

While there are some great collage artists who have created stunning works of enormous complexity (Kurt Schwitters, for example), it's difficult to carry that off. My own experience has led me to believe that with collage less is indeed more. The openness and simplicity of the "starter" collages in this collection are evidence of that.

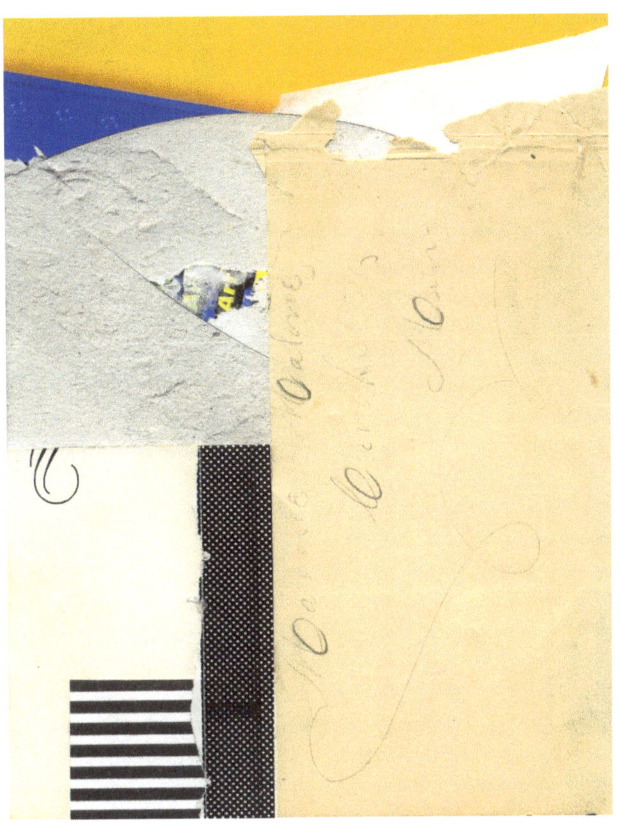

In this collage, for example, Zach has layered a very few elements in such a way that the echoes and contrasts among the shapes and textures and colors and lines create a world of startling depth and richness. Like each of the other collages in *Acute Angles*, it invites us to step inside and stay a while, to experience the harmonies (and discordances), to immerse ourselves in the world of the collage in order to return to our own world refreshed and reawakened.

Bruce Schauble
March 2016

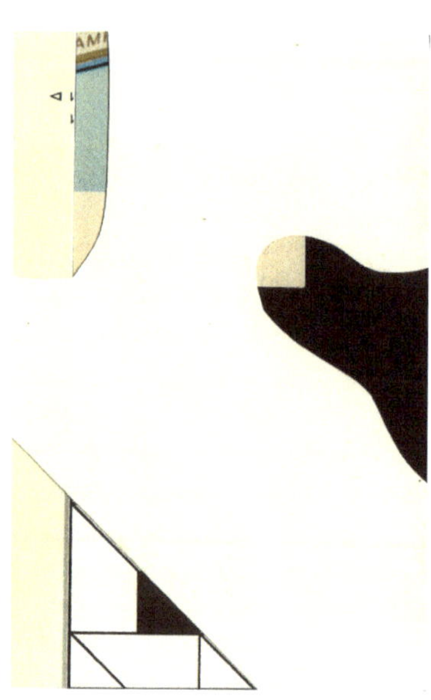

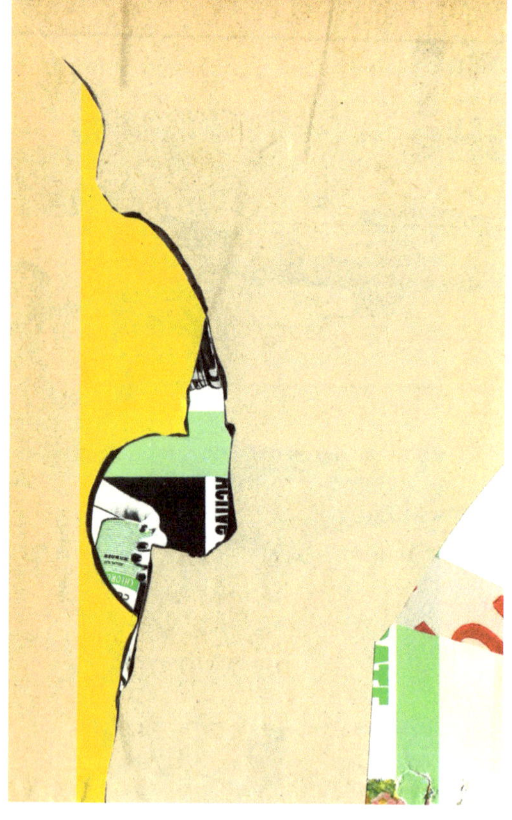
VALID

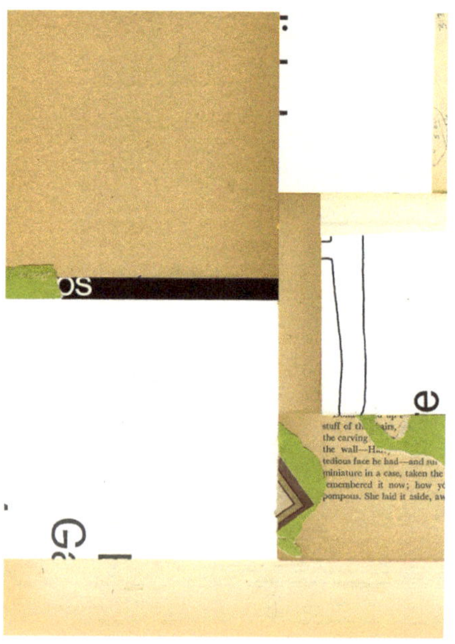
os
e
stuff of th   ain,
the carving
the wall—H
tedious face he had—and su
miniature in a case, taken the
emembered it now; how yo
pompous. She laid it aside, aw
G

137
43
ek
re nothing mattered
other, the loveli
stretching b
ng back
re we b
ne to
ie
ner

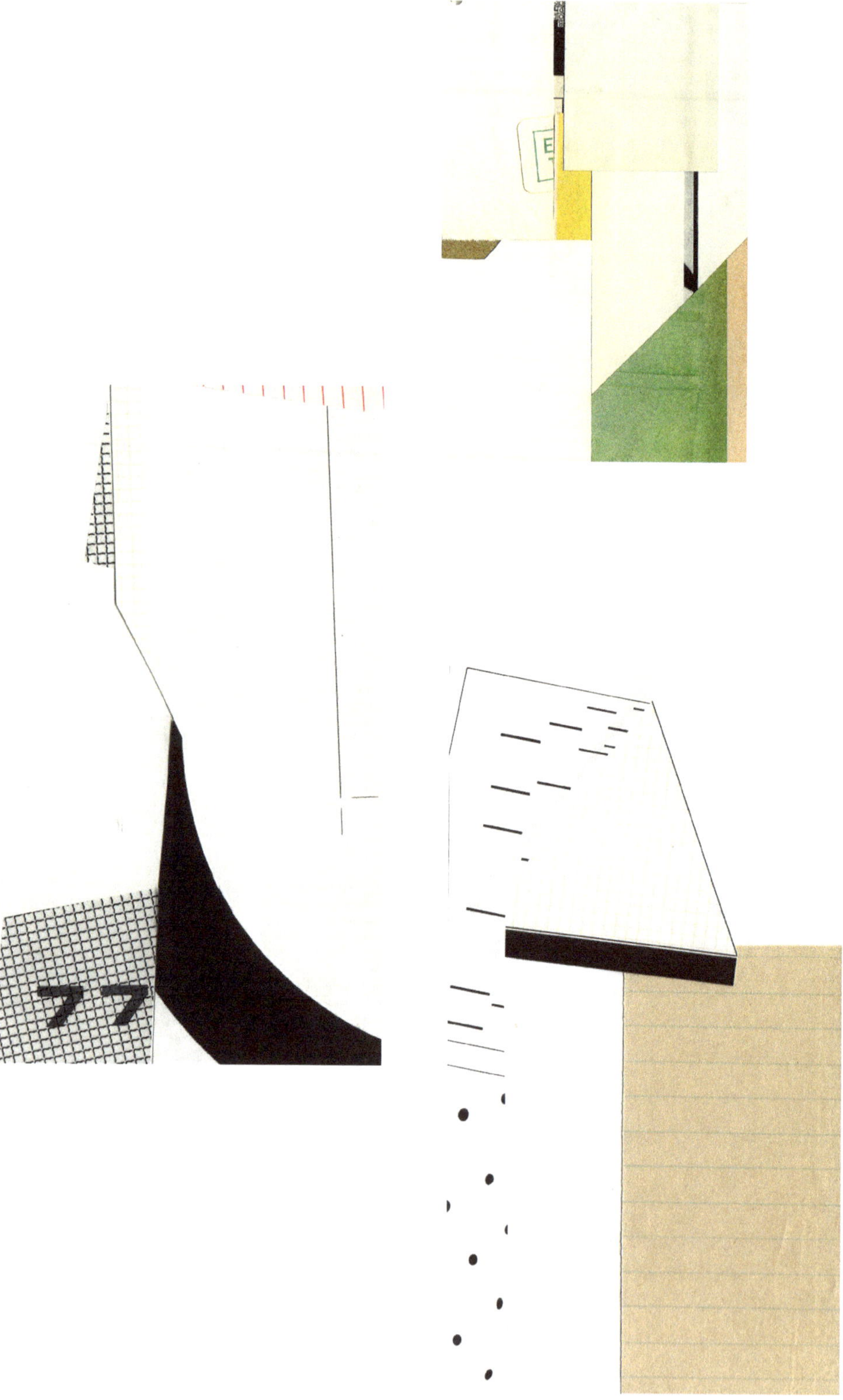

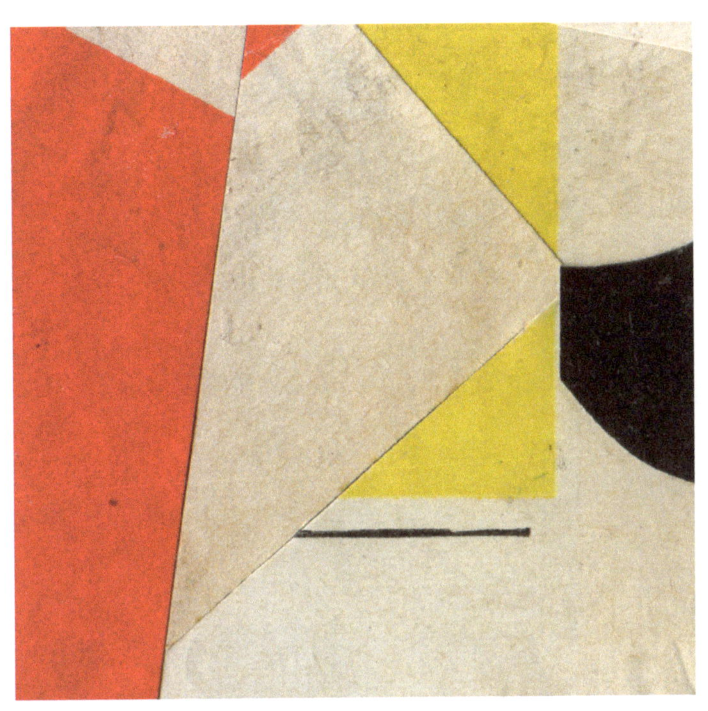

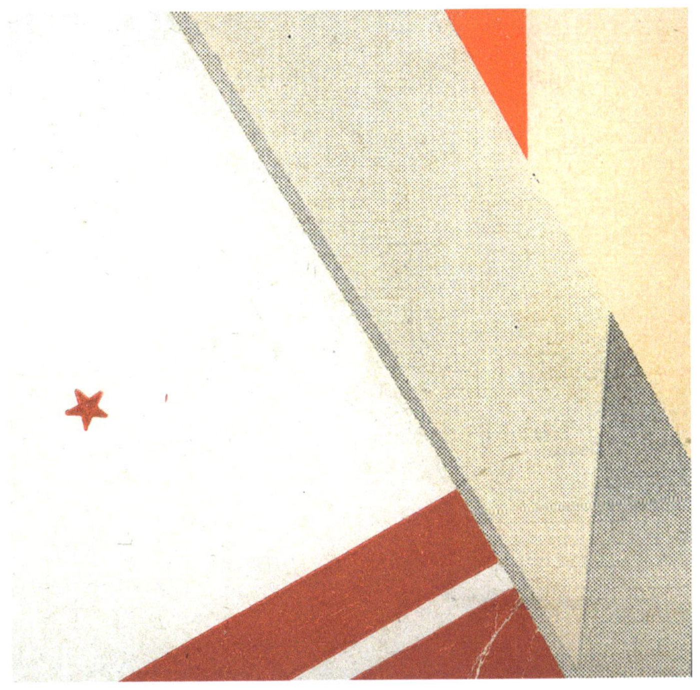

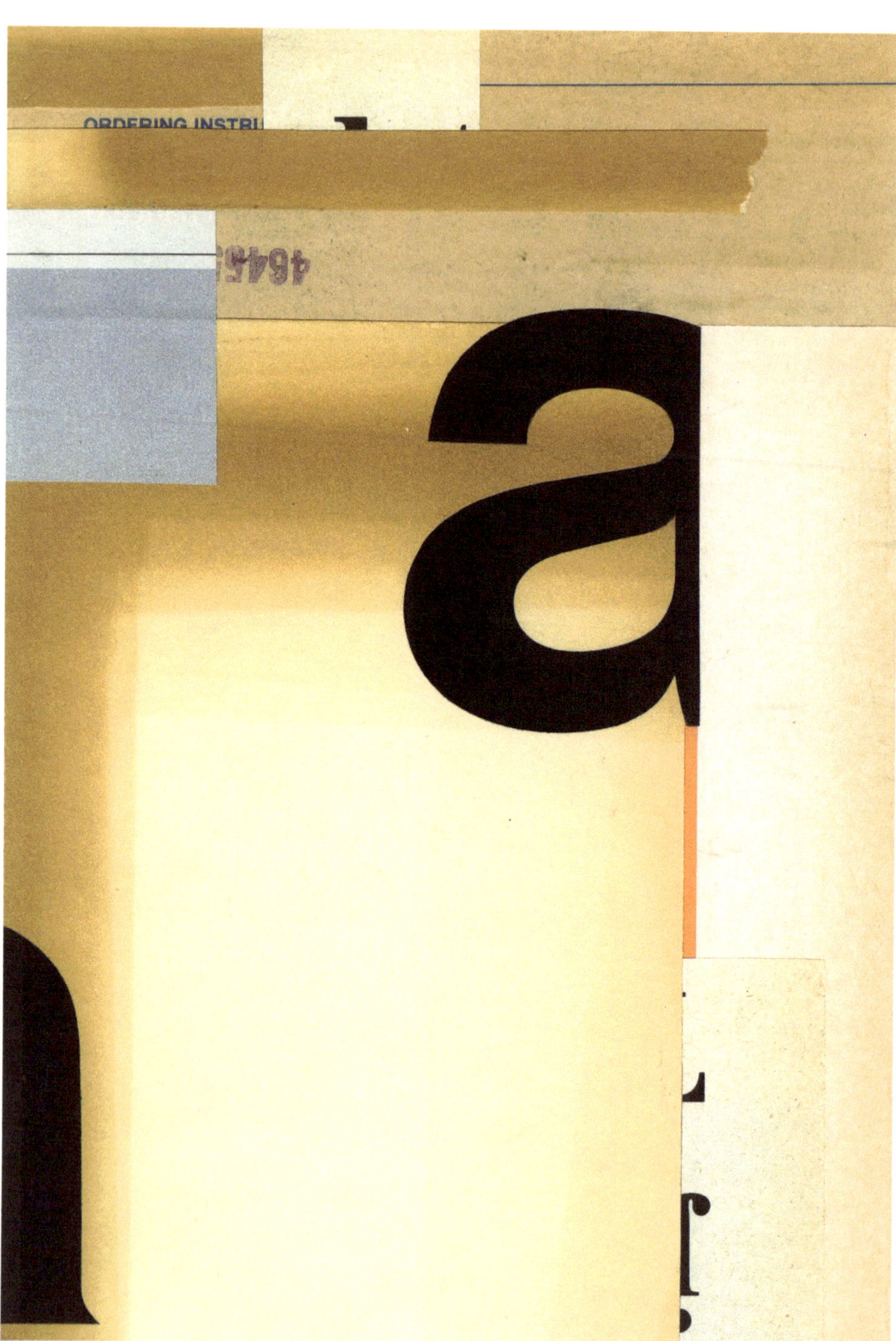

ORDERING INSTRU
4645

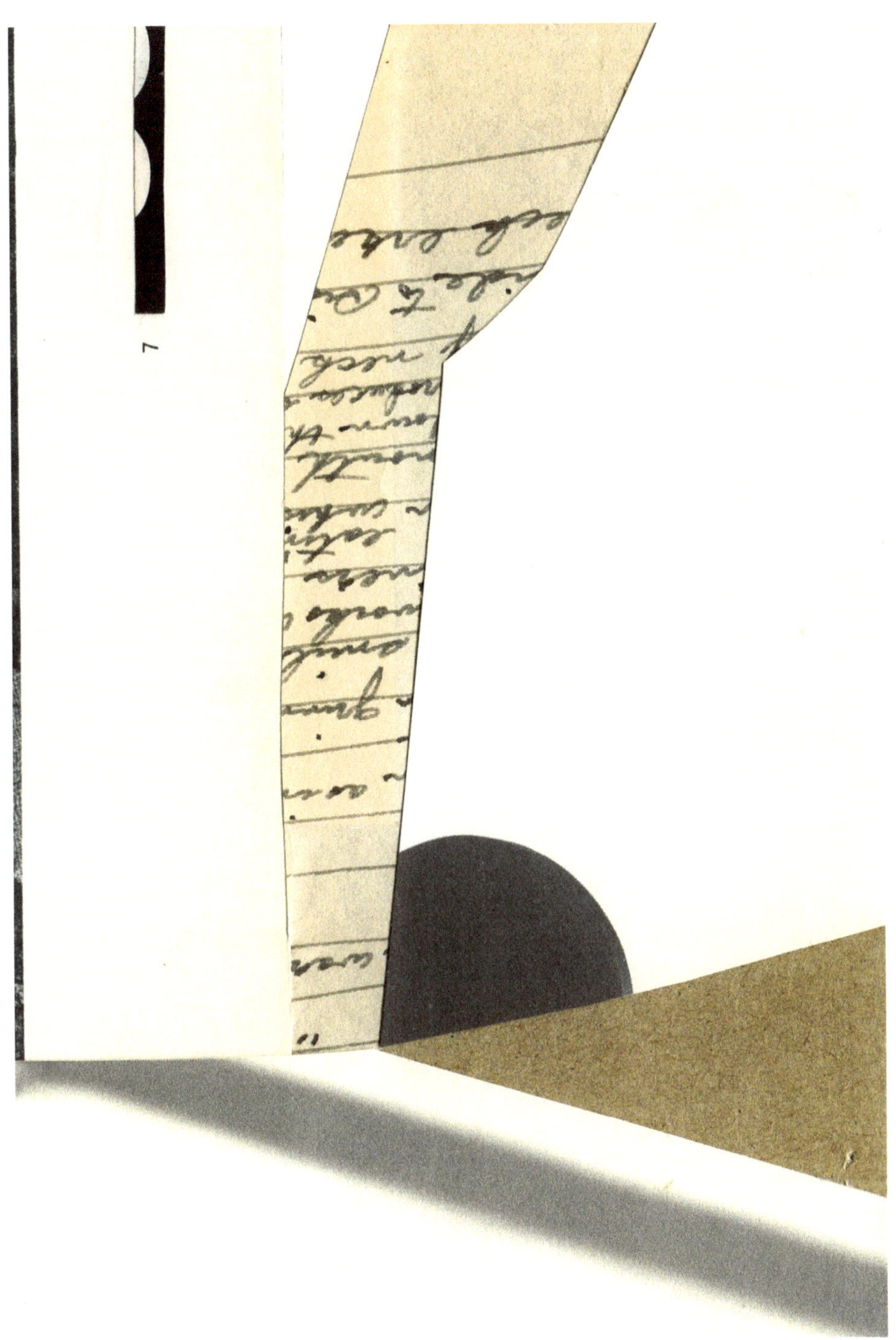

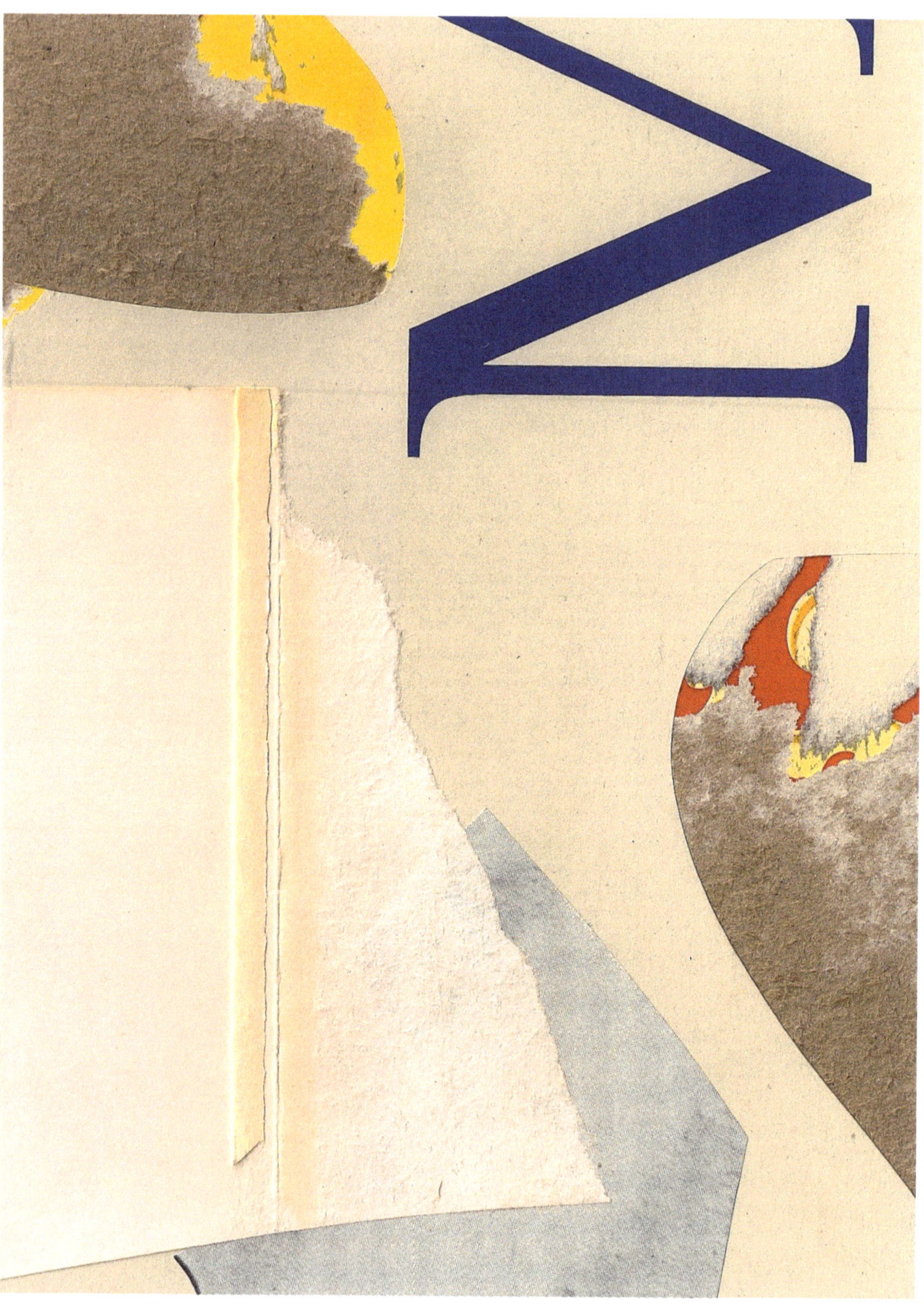

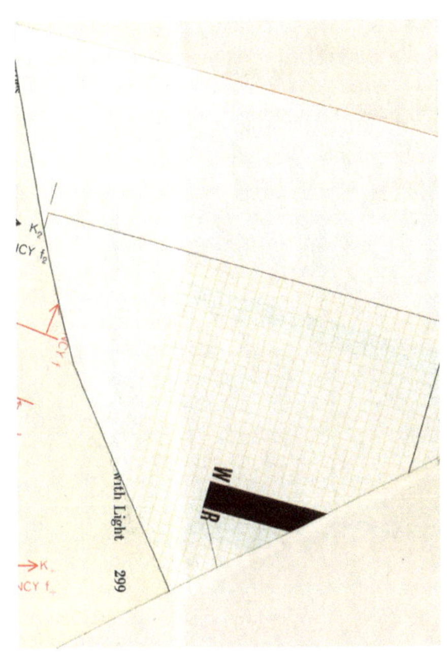

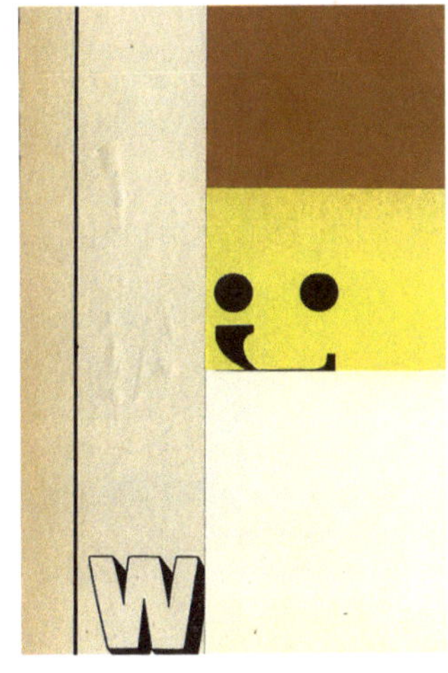

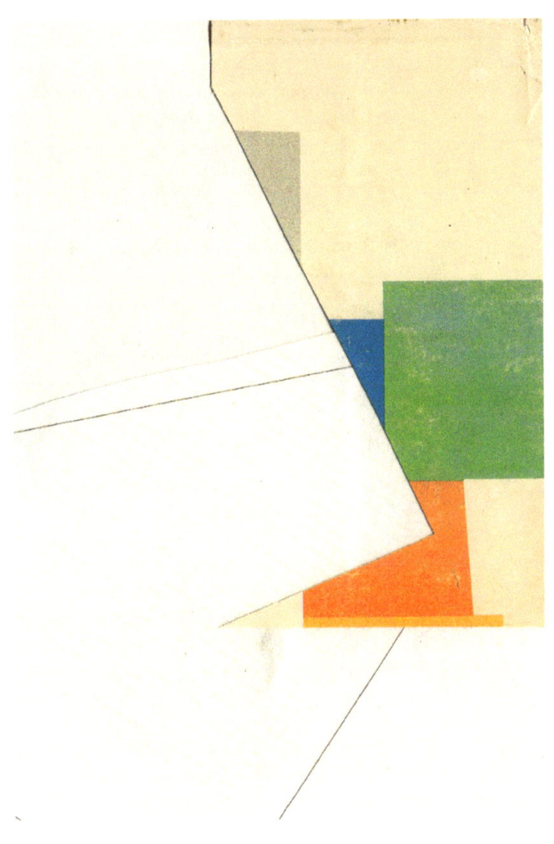

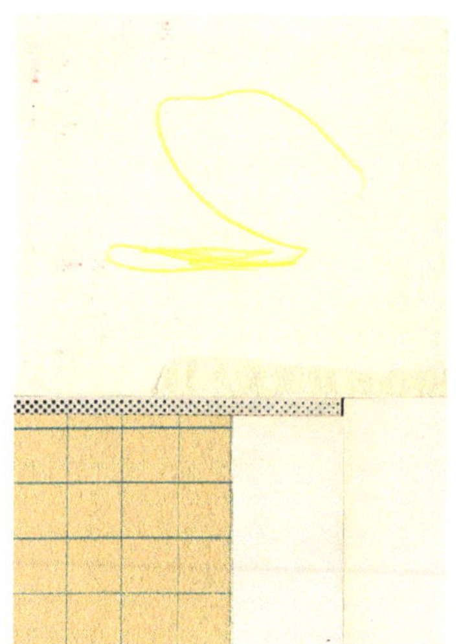

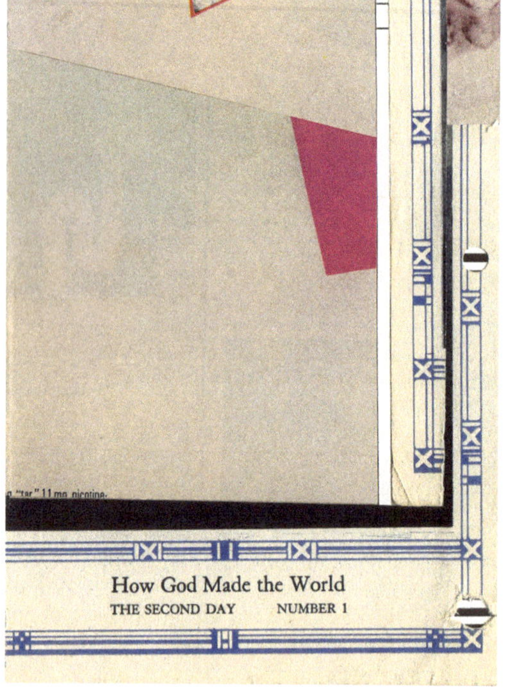

How God Made the World
THE SECOND DAY   NUMBER 1

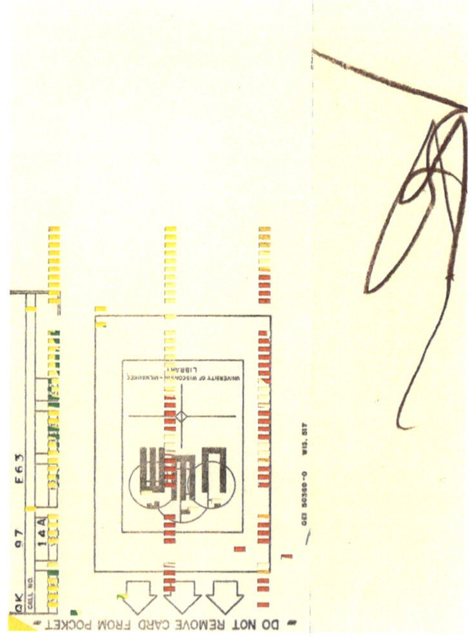

UNIVERSITY OF WISCONSIN—MILWAUKEE
LIBRARY
DO NOT REMOVE CARD FROM POCKET

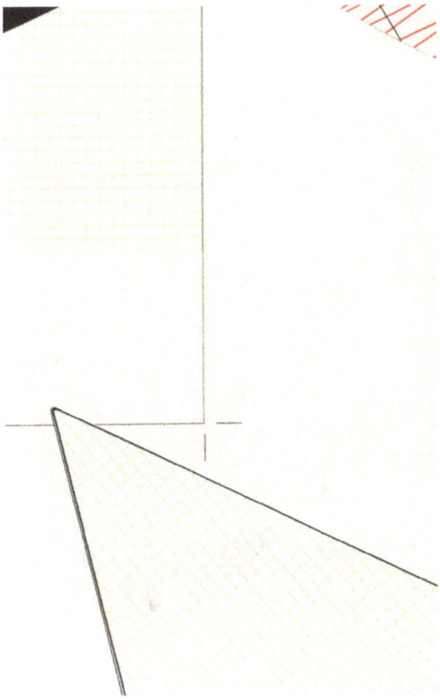

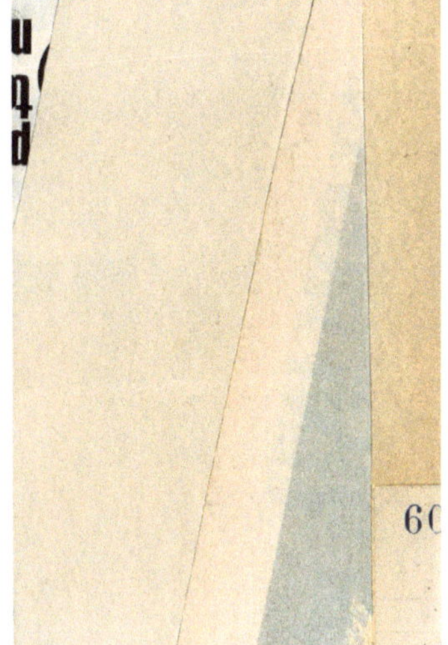

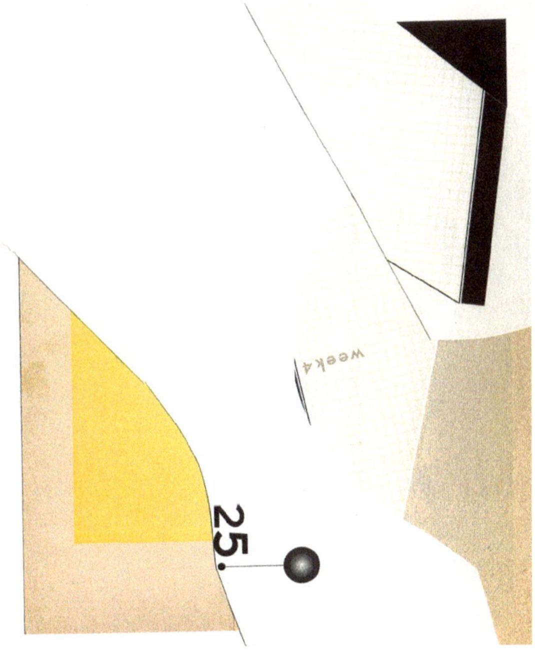

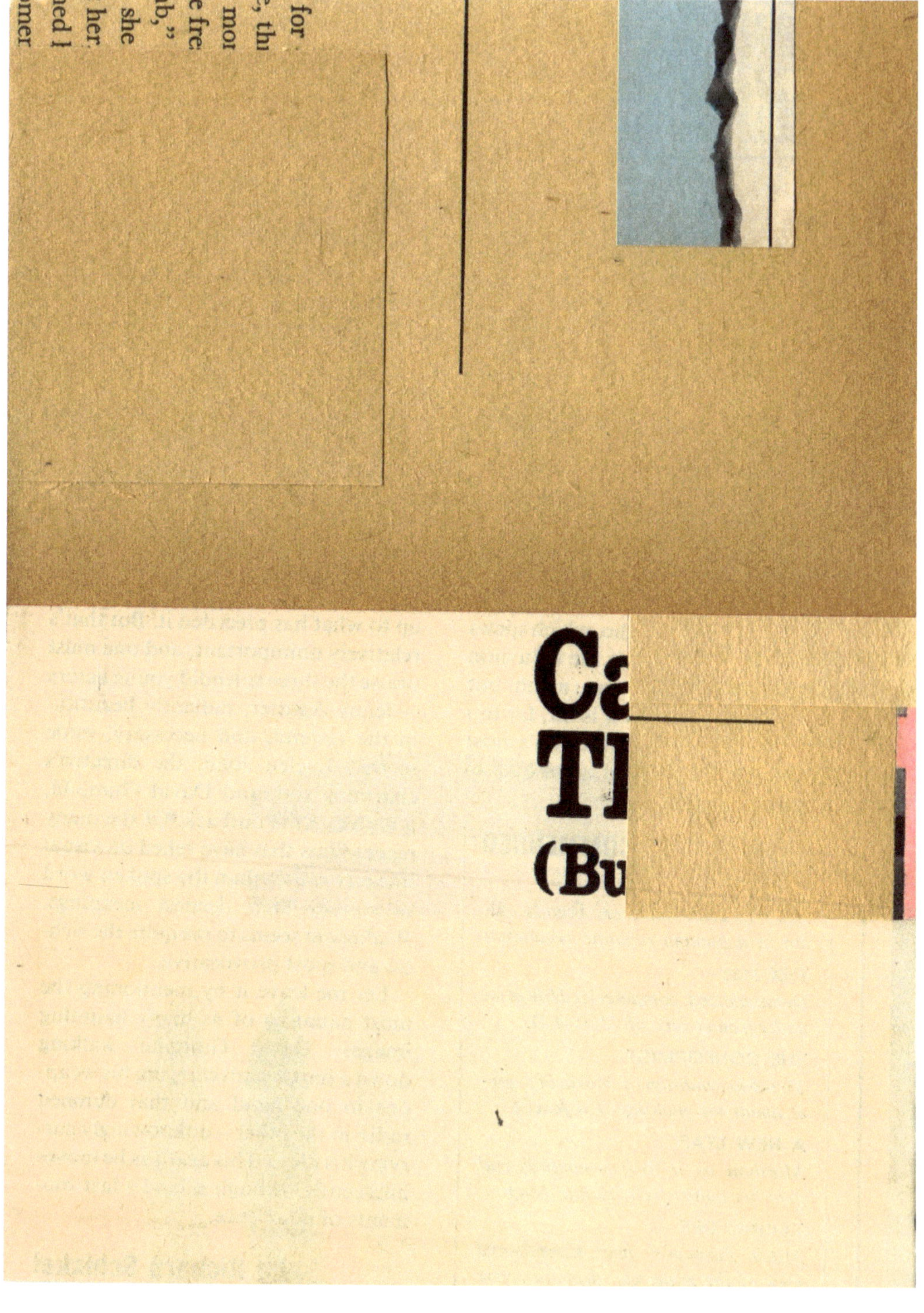
Ca
TI
(Bu
for
e, thi
moi
e fre
b,"
she
her
ned l
omer

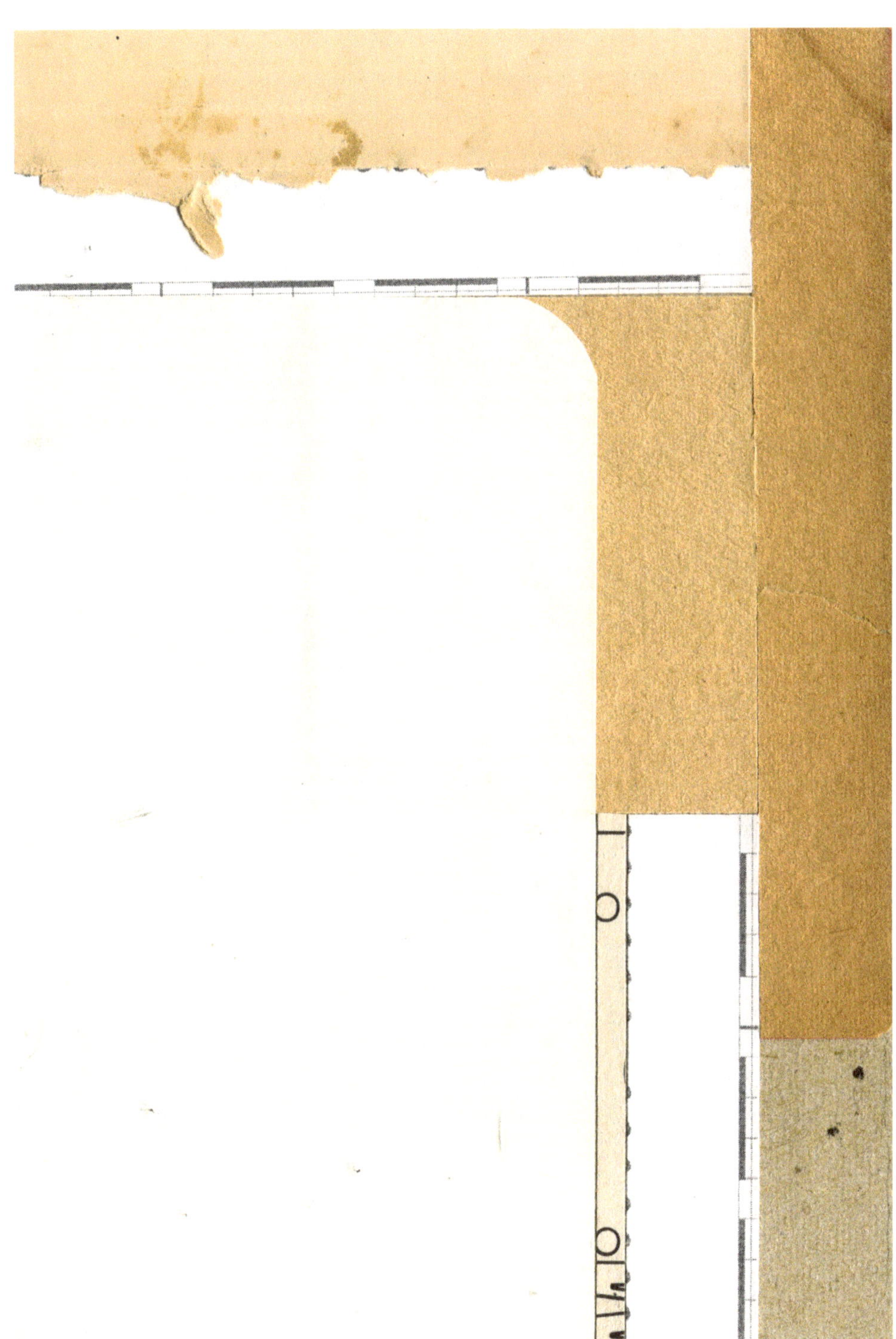

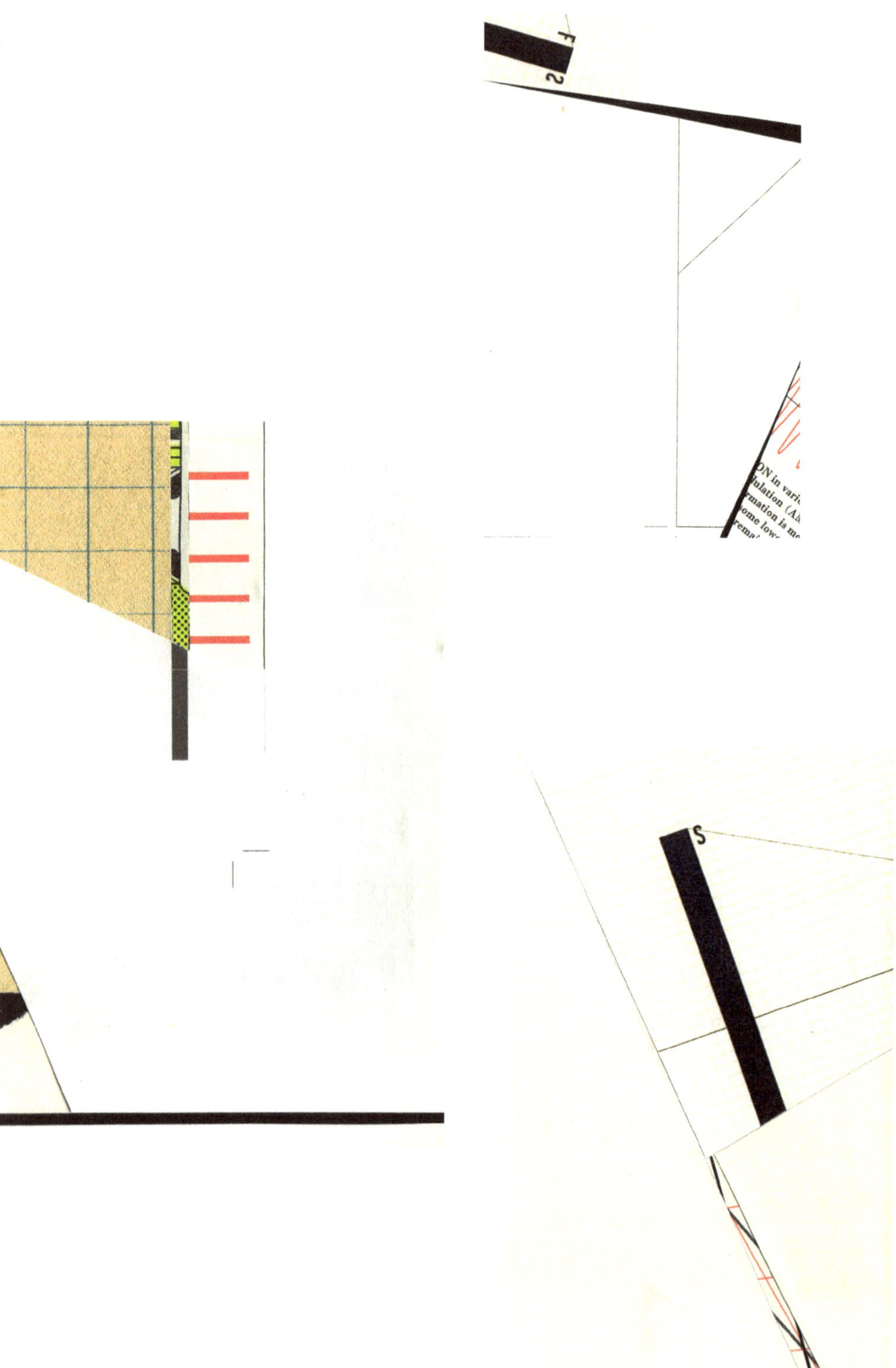
ON in vari
ulation (A
rmation is m
ome low
rems

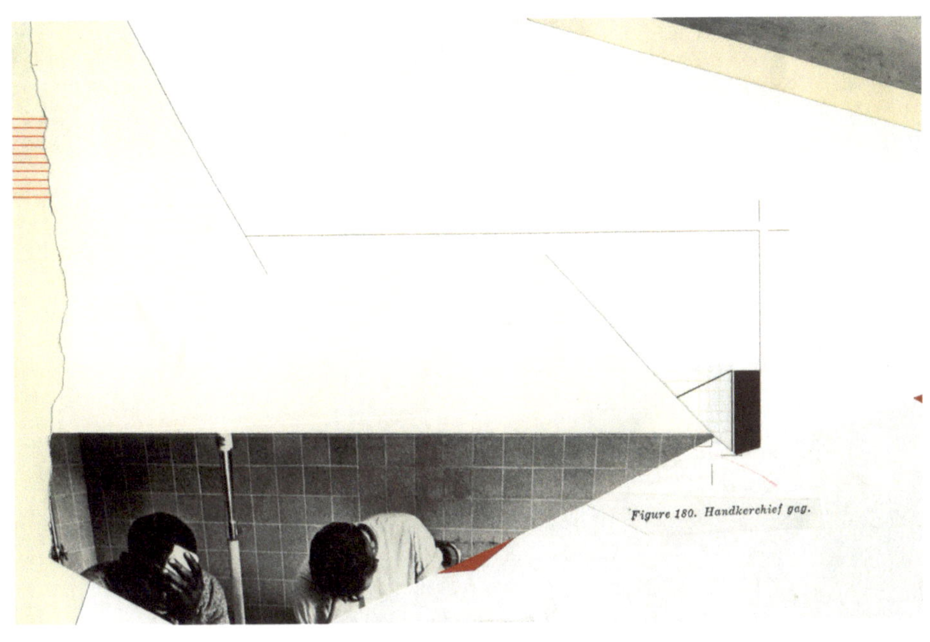

Figure 180. Handkerchief gag.

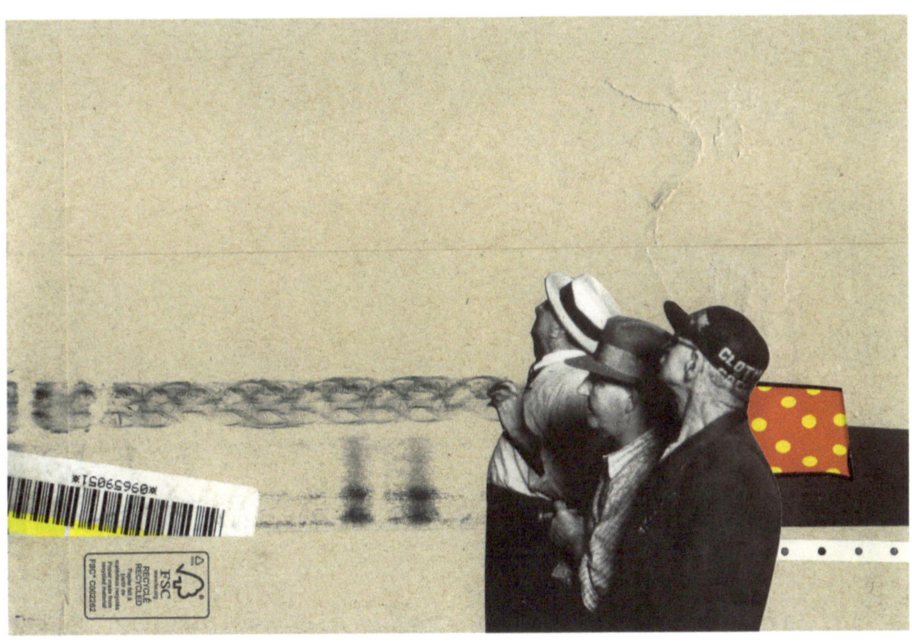

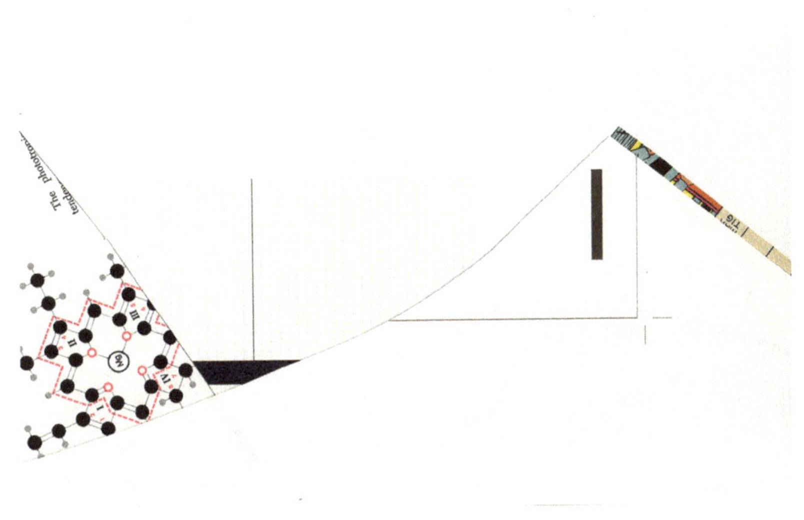

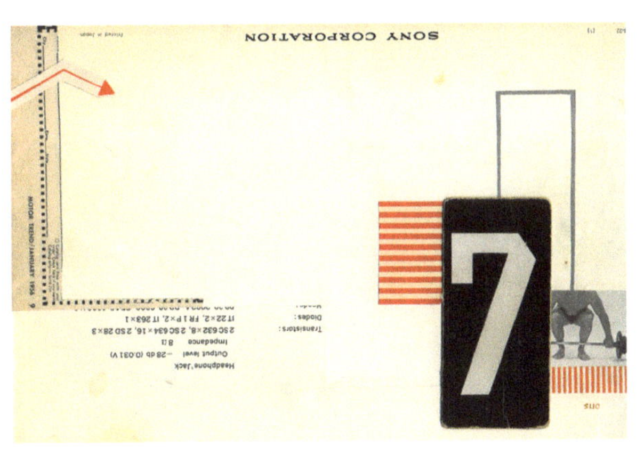
SONY CORPORATION
Printed in Japan
MONTH TREND / JANUARY 1956
Headphone Jack
Output level   —28 db (0.031 V)
Impedance   8 Ω
Transistors: 2SC632×8, 2SC634×16, 2SD28×3
Diodes: 1T22×2, FR1 IP×2, 1T263×1

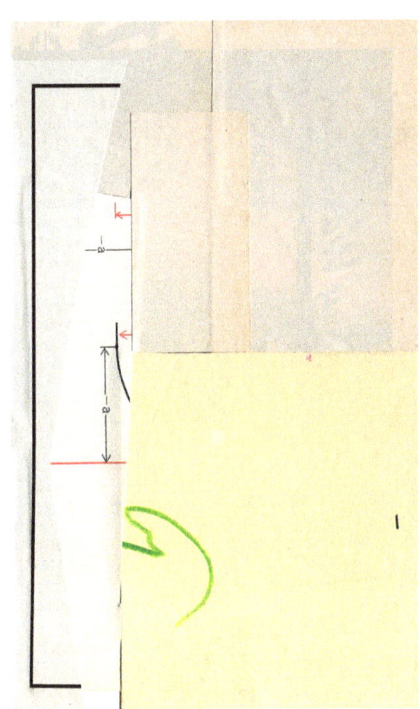

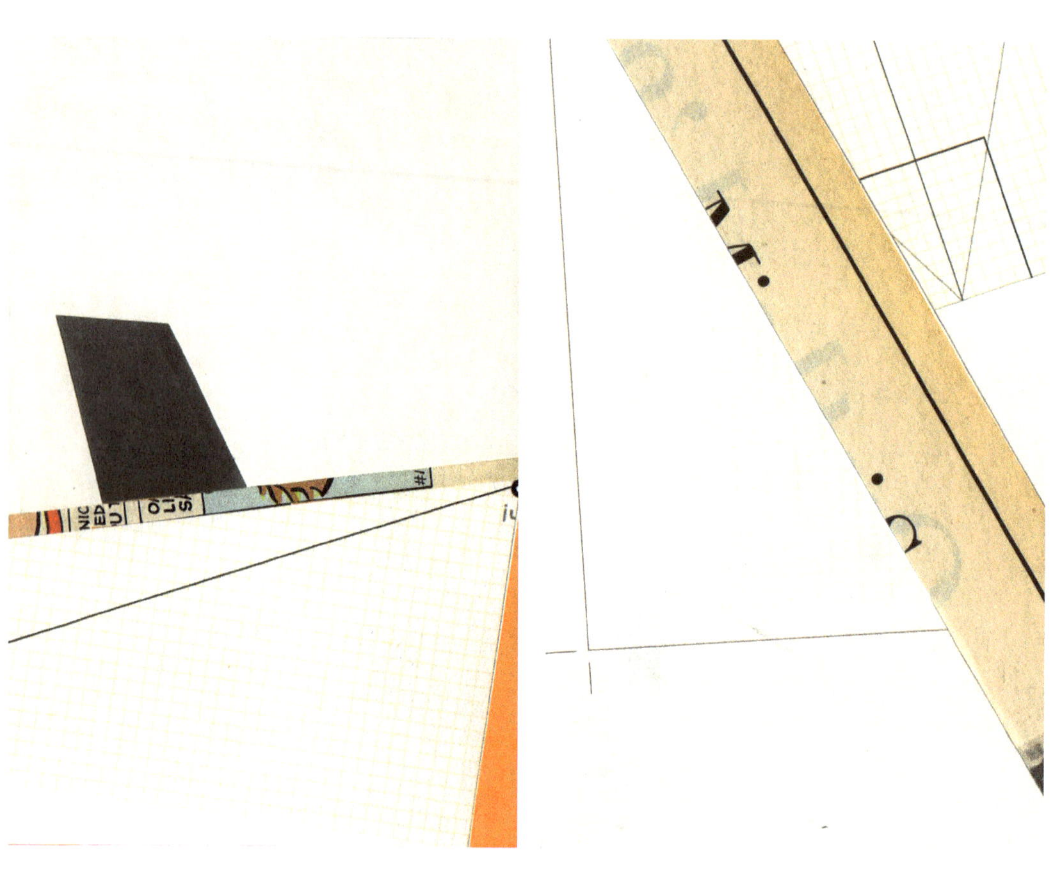

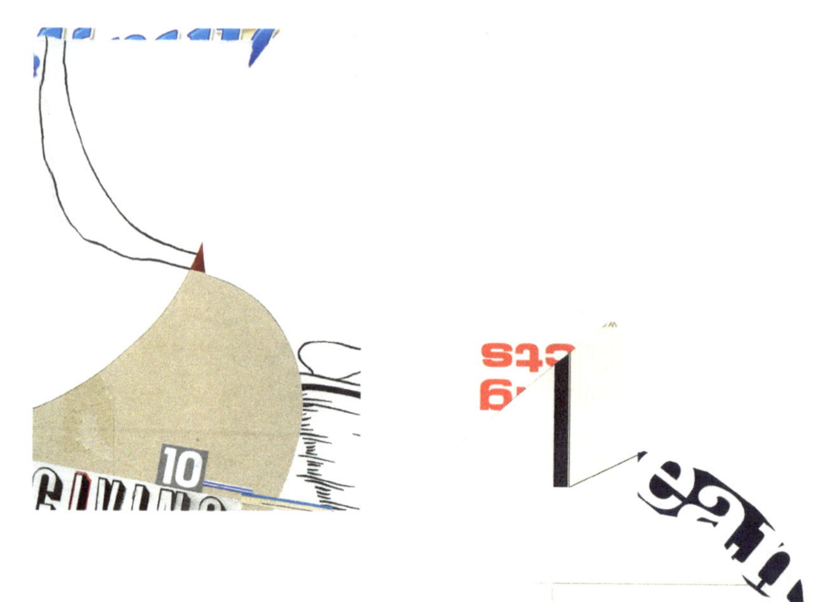

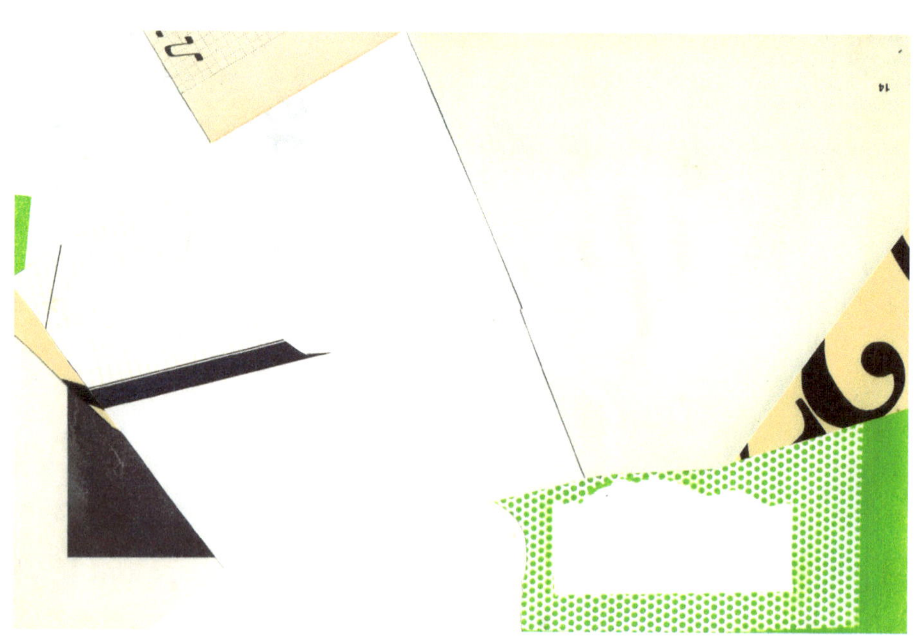

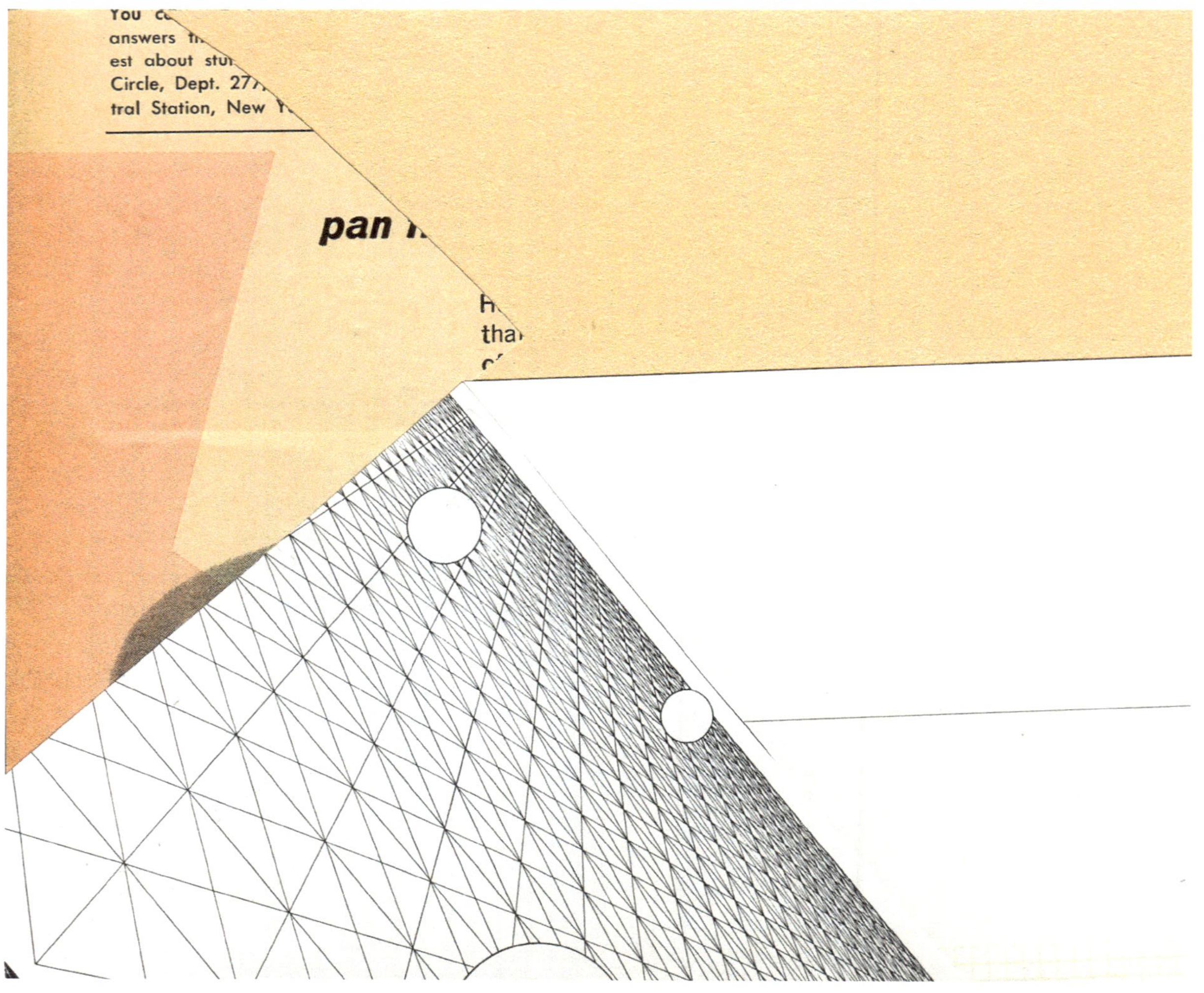

You c
answers h
est about stu
Circle, Dept. 27
tral Station, New Y
pan
H
tha

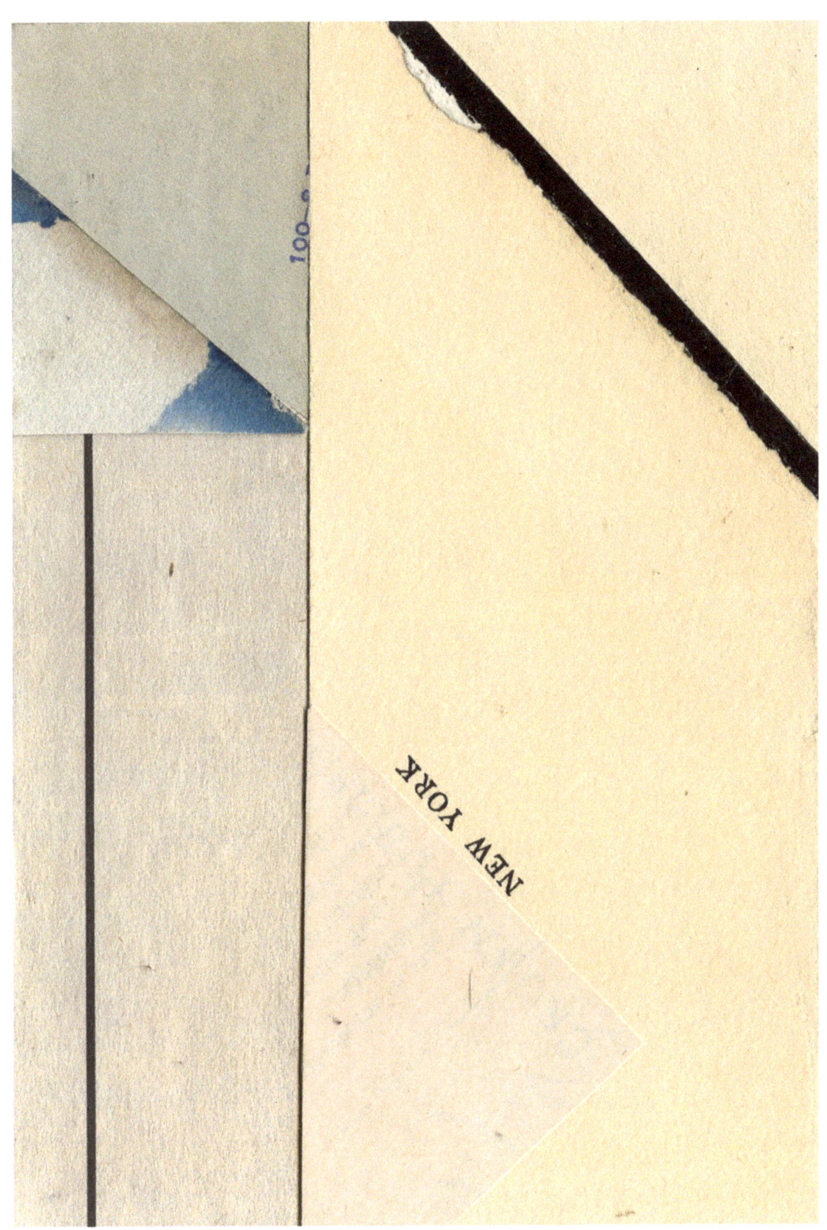

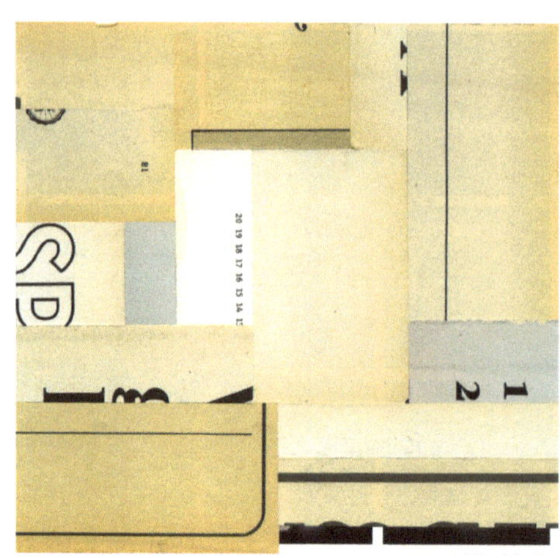

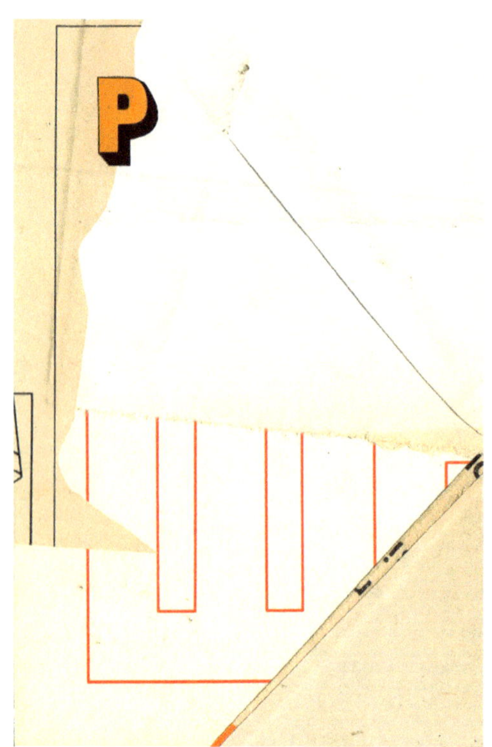

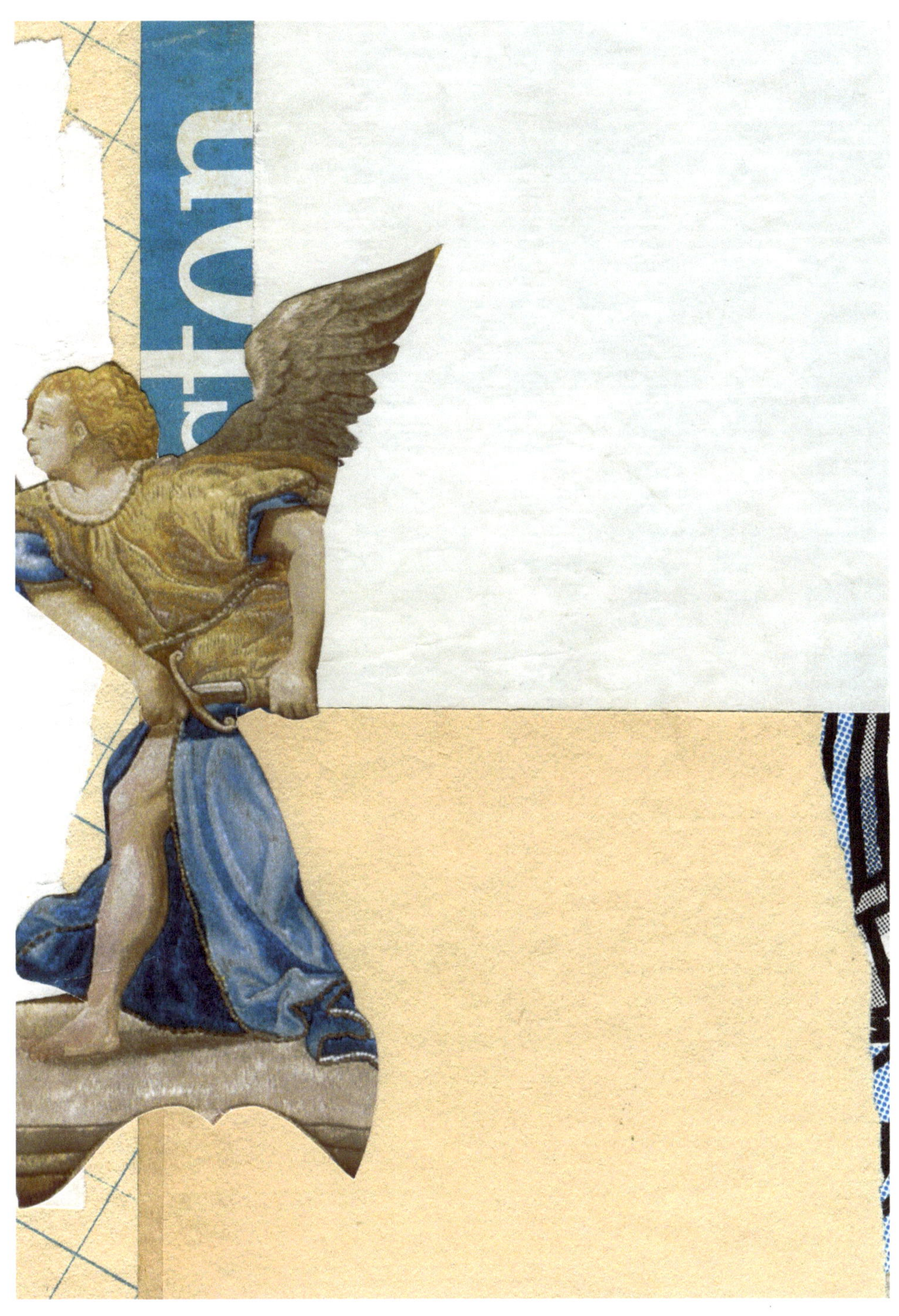

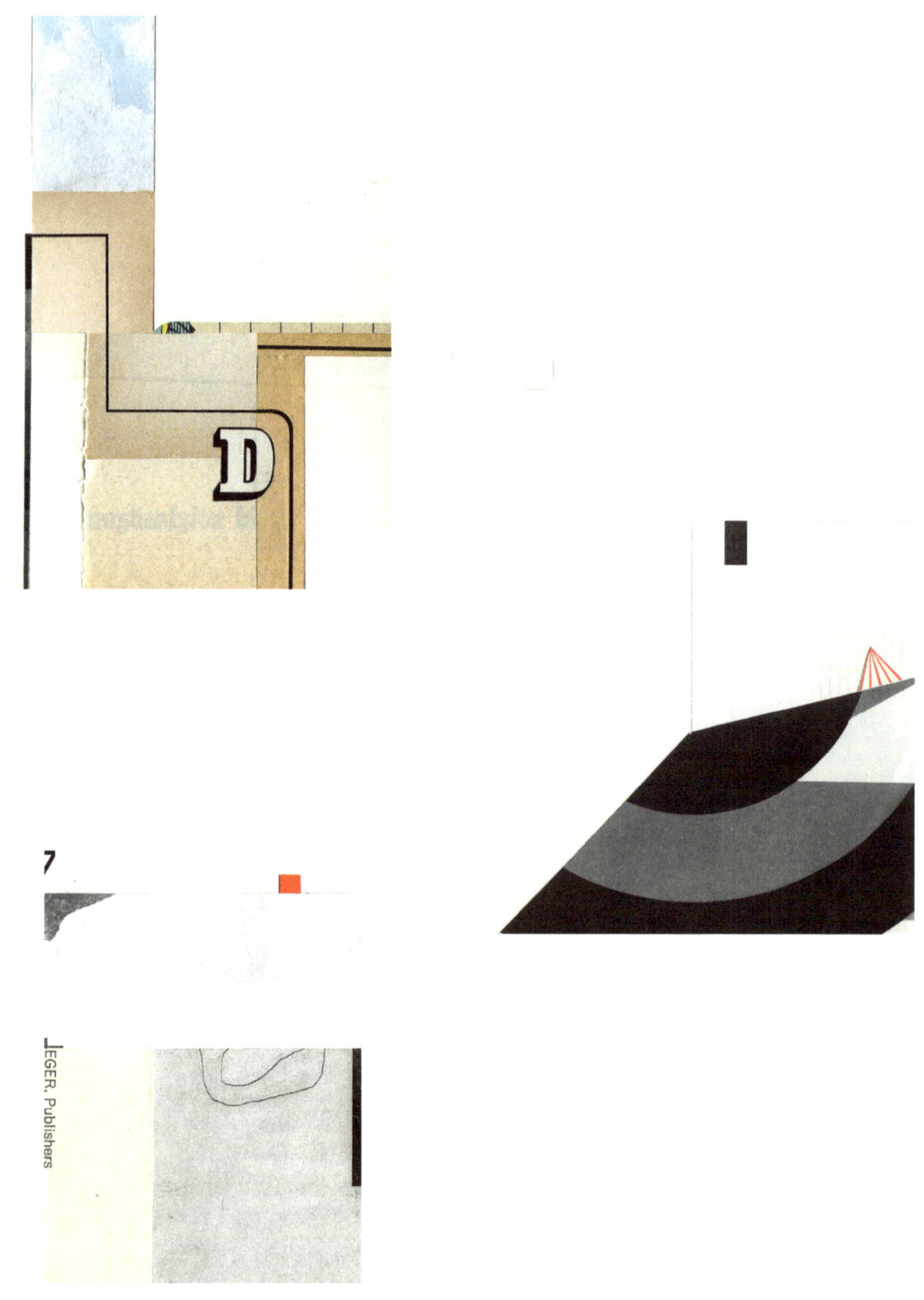
D
7
EGER, Publishers

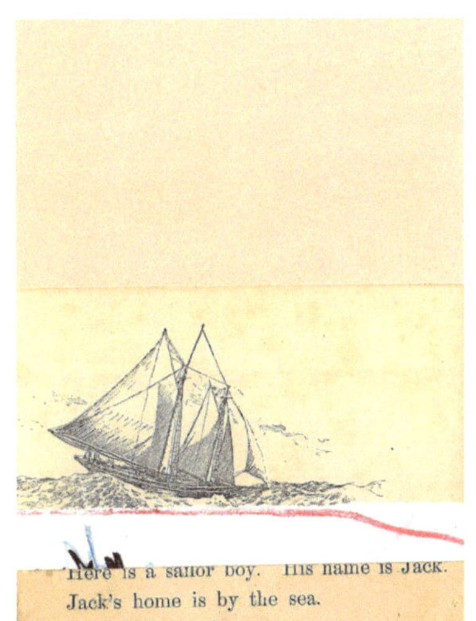

Here is a sailor boy. His name is Jack.
Jack's home is by the sea.
He loves the sea.

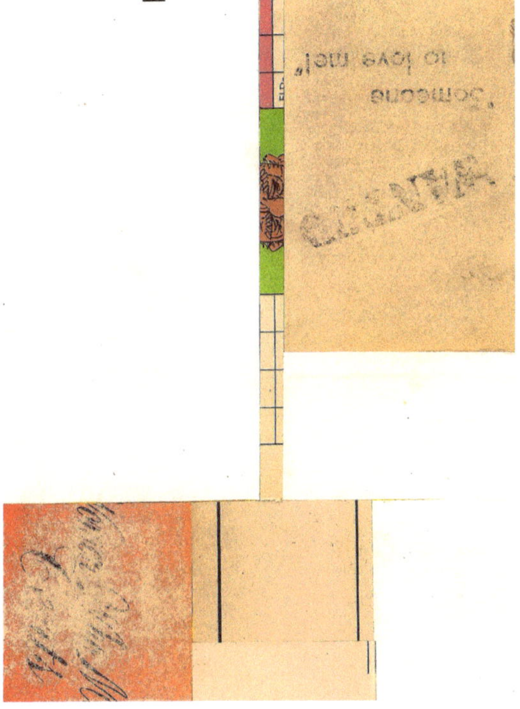

to love me!"
Someone
CANADA

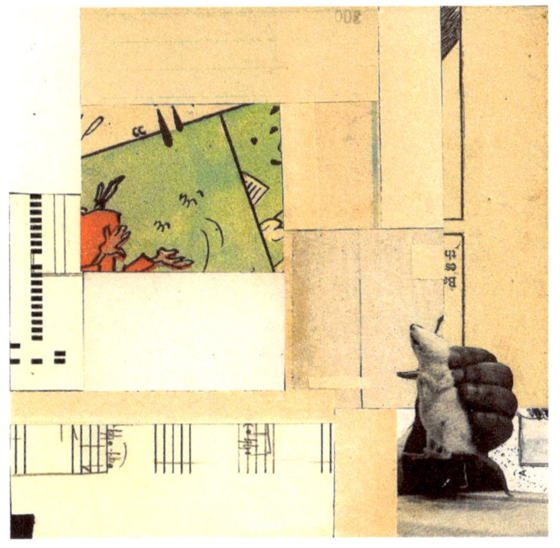

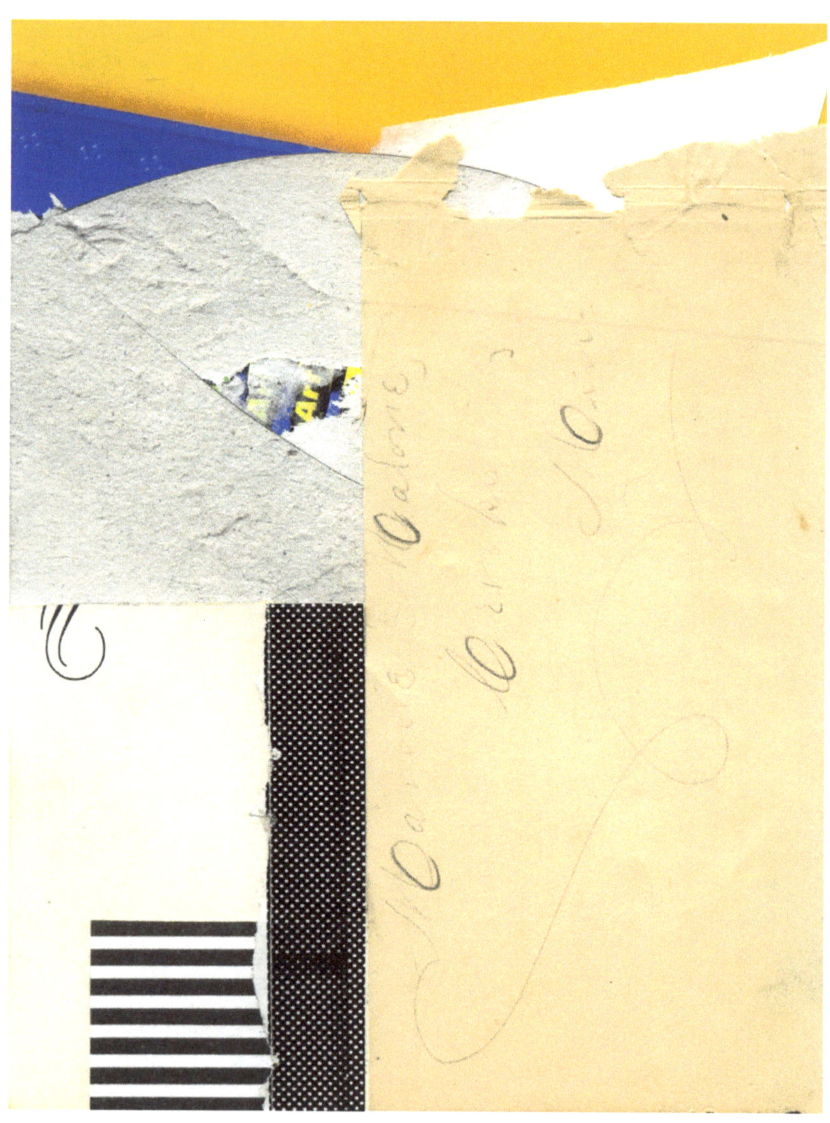

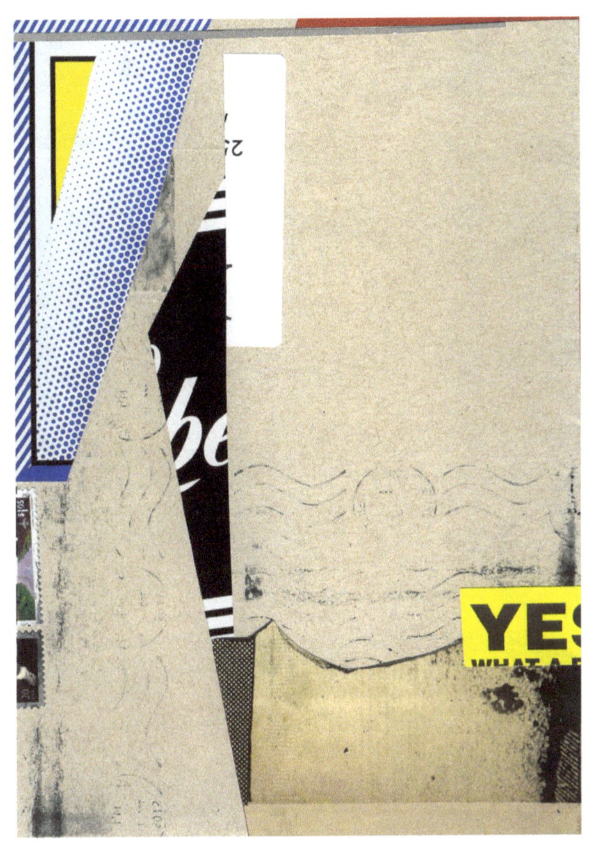

YES
WHAT A

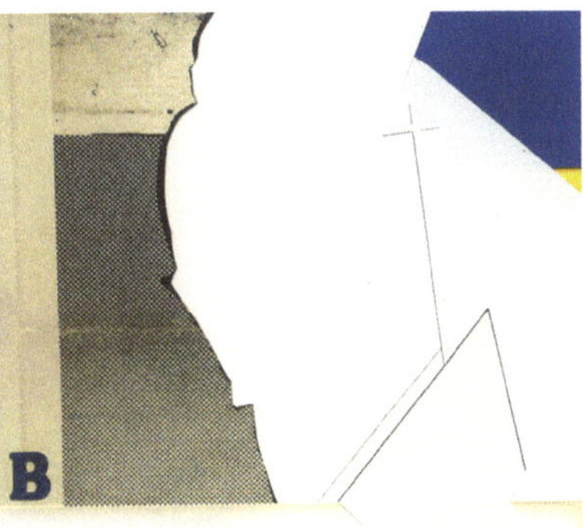

B

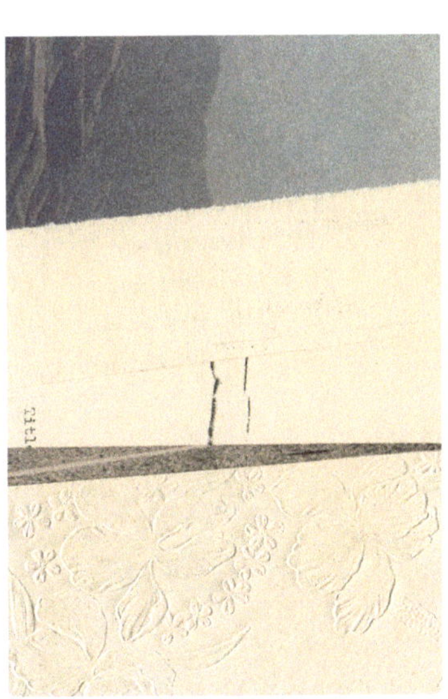

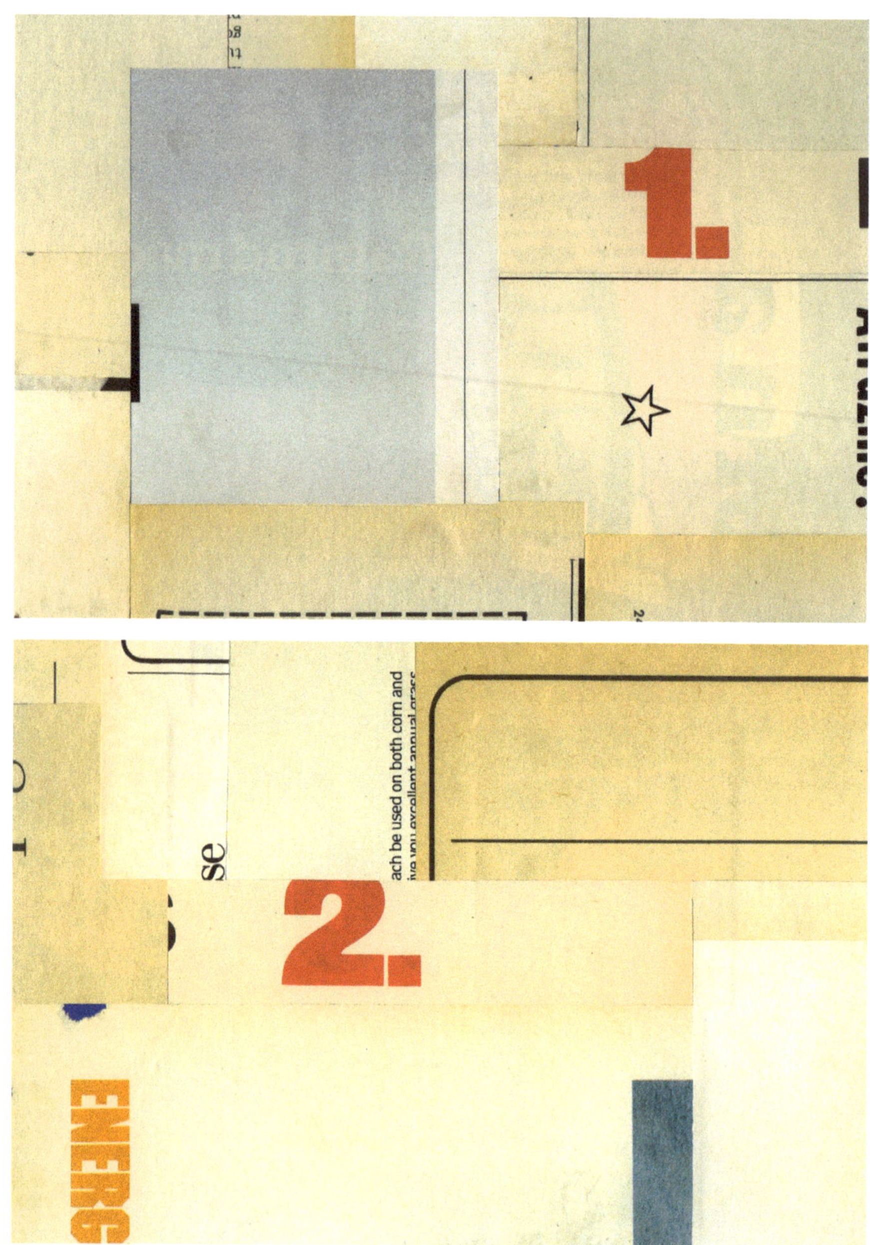
1.
2.
ENERG

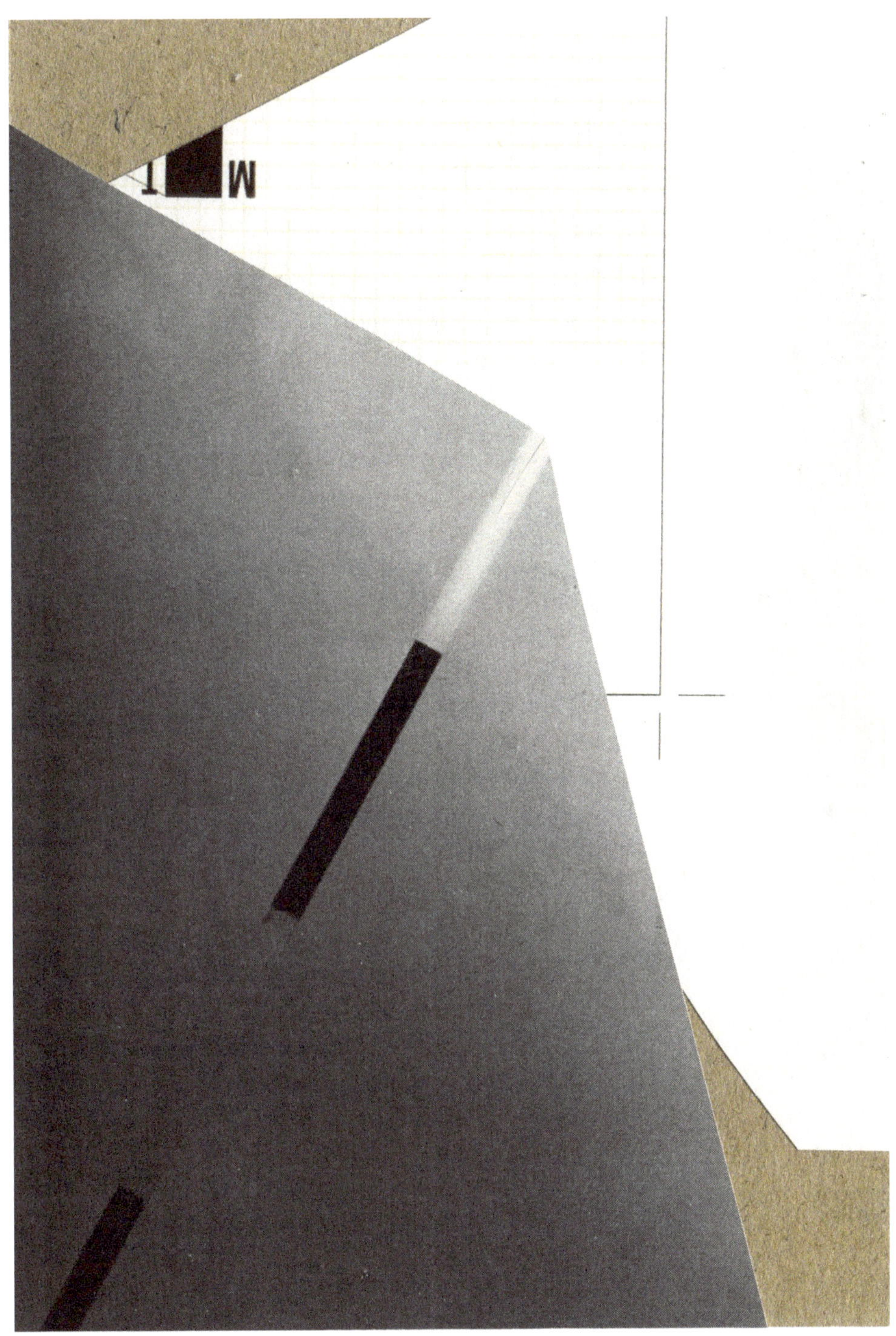

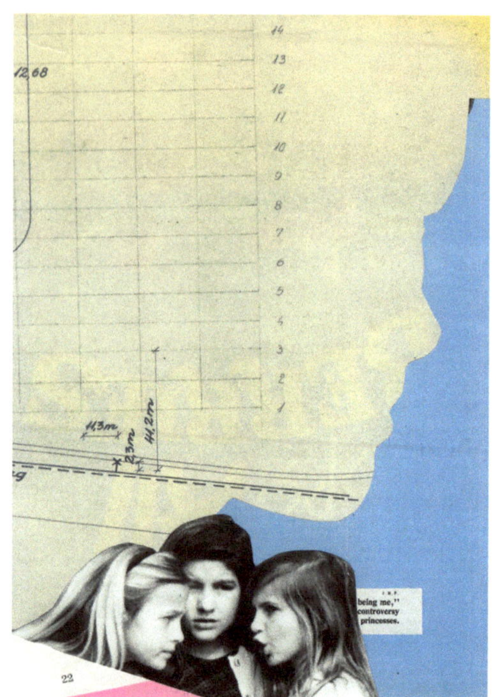

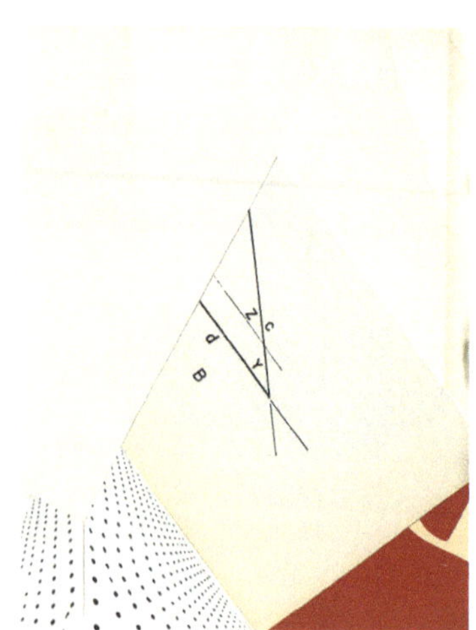

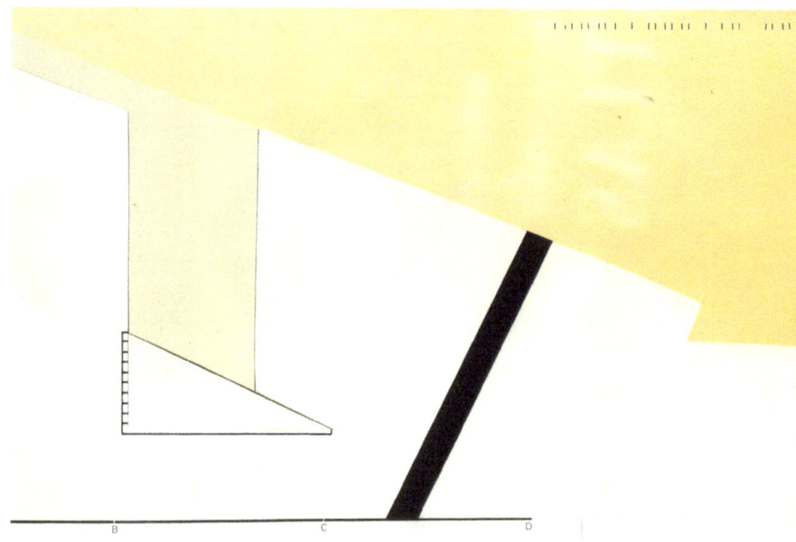

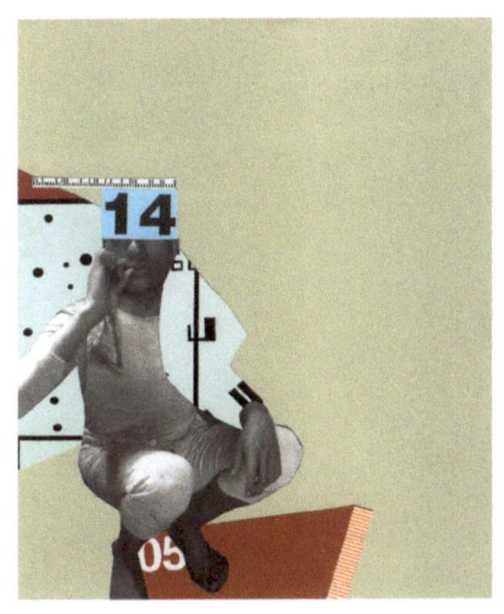
14
05

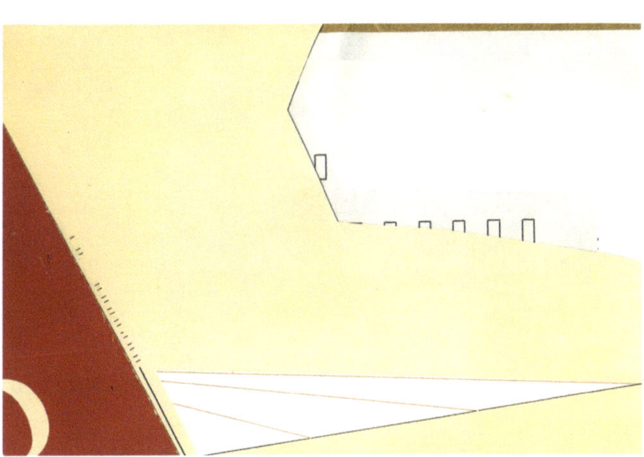

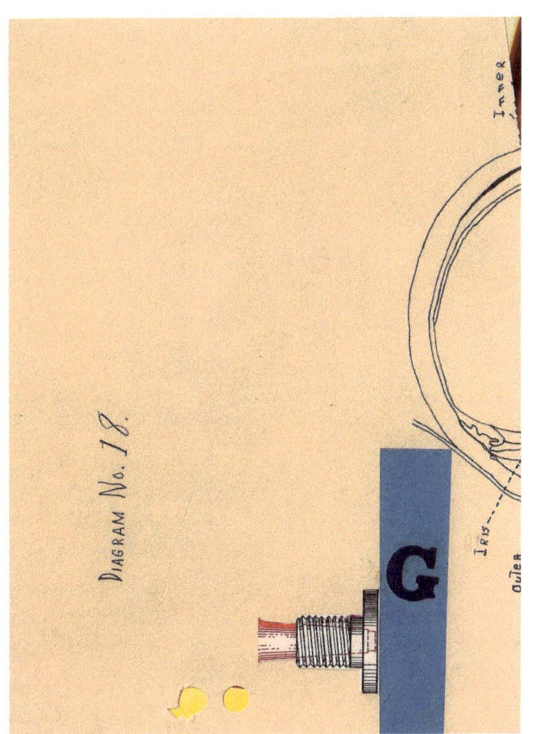
DIAGRAM No. 18.
Inner
Iris
Outer
G

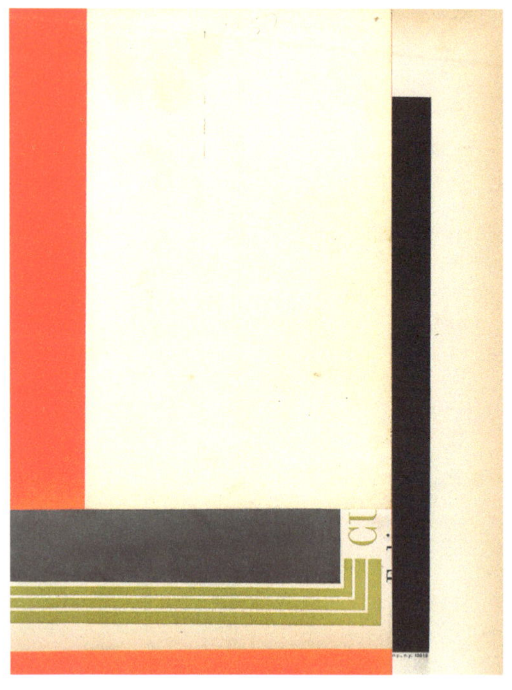

m. Apr 4 — 1899

Time-Sav
of those who
equally usefu
nance engine
or maintain
The editor
ists, many of
contributed t
21277
. . . . I still be

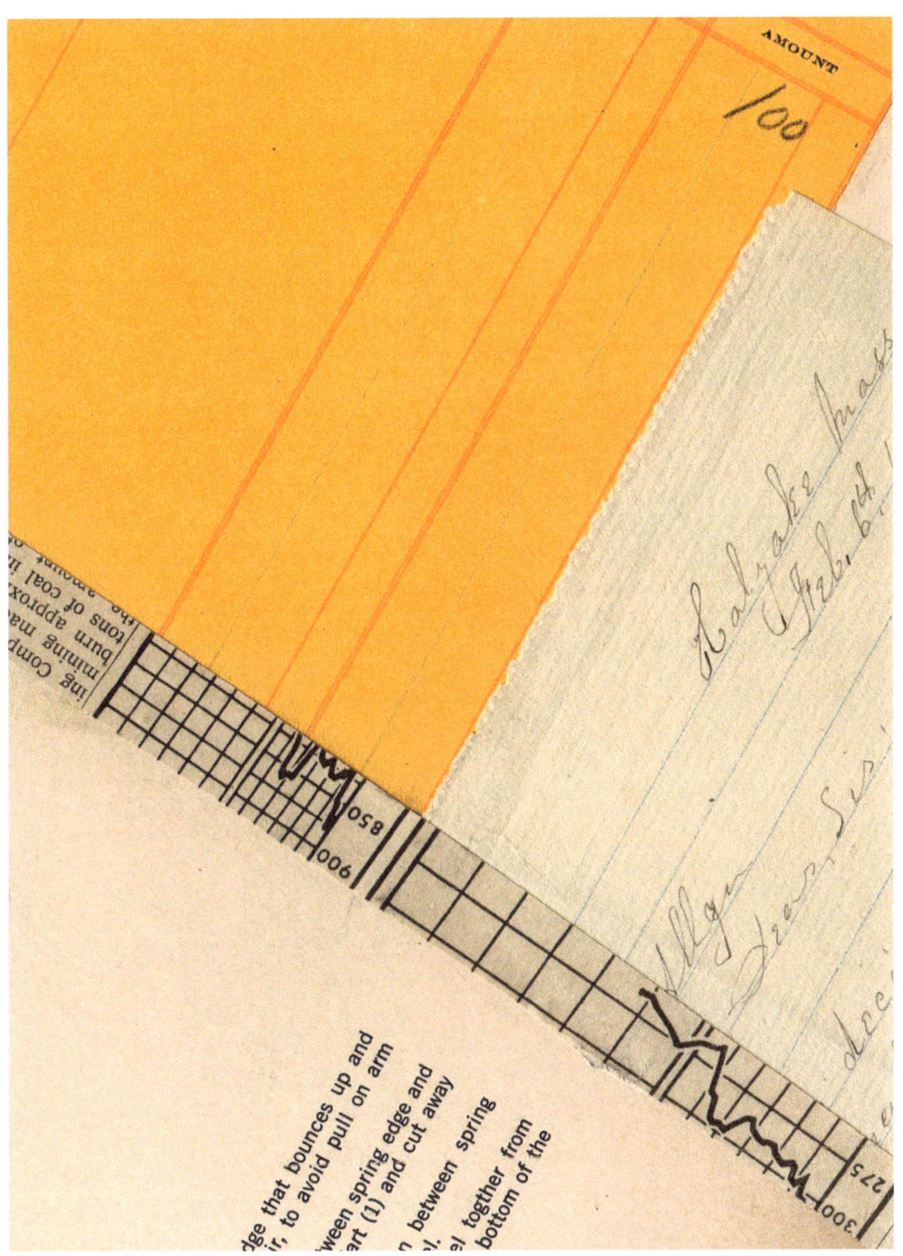

AMOUNT
100

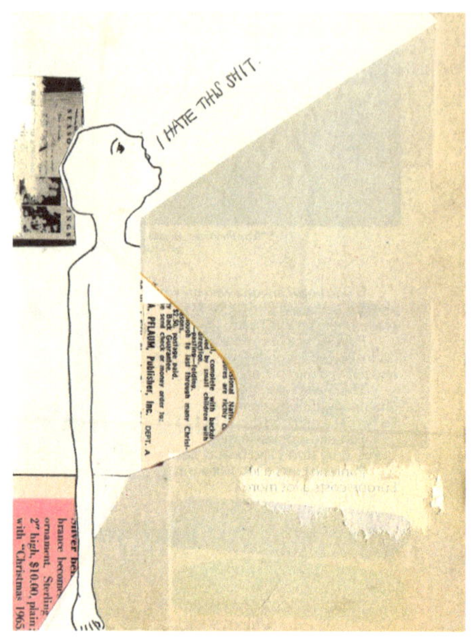
I HATE THIS SHIT.

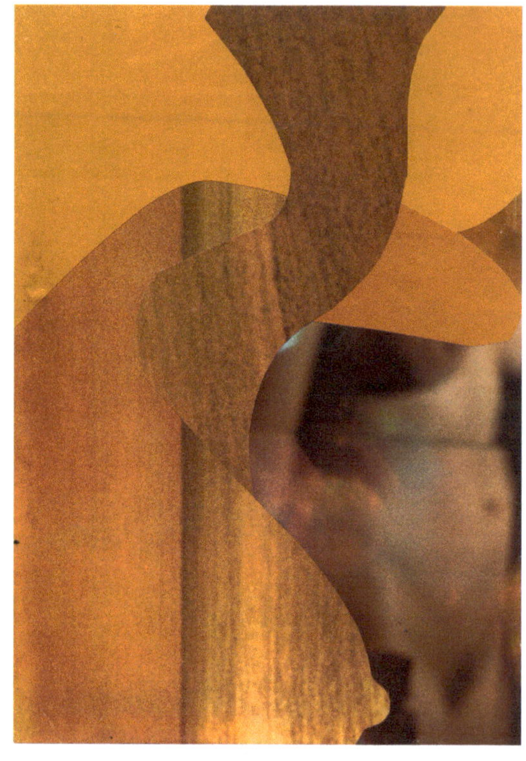

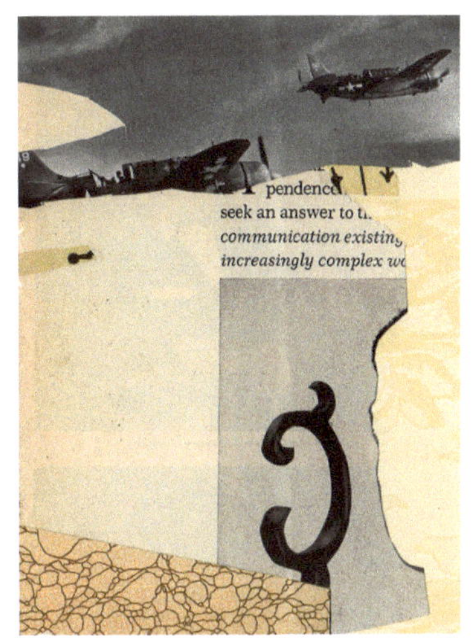
pendence
seek an answer to t
communication existing
increasingly complex wo

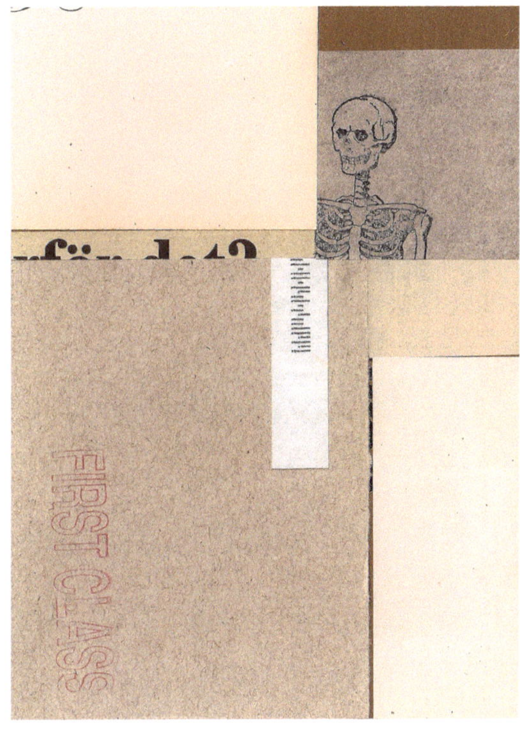
FIRST CLASS

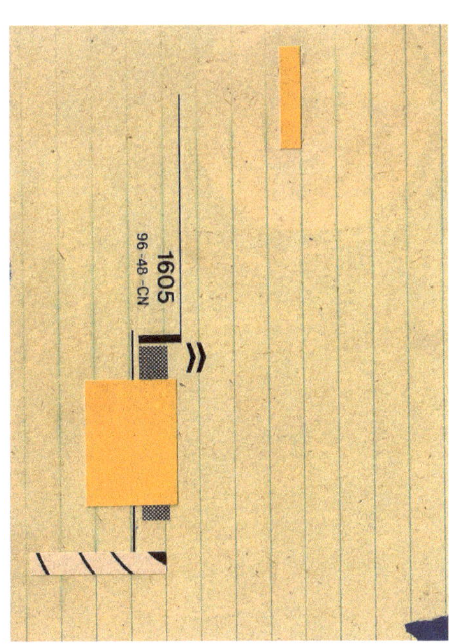
1605
96 -48 -CN

www.ingramcontent.com/pod-product-compliance
Lightning Source LLC
Chambersburg PA
CBHW041233050726
47599CB00007B/933